The
HEARTLAND
COMPANION

The HEARTLAND COMPANION

Beth Franks

MALLARD PRESS
An imprint of
BDD Promotional Book Company, Inc.
666 Fifth Avenue
New York, New York 10103

A TERN ENTERPRISE BOOK

Published by MALLARD PRESS
An Imprint of BDD Promotional Book Company, Inc.
666 Fifth Avenue
New York, New York 10103

Mallard Press and its accompanying design and logo are trademarks of BDD Promotional Book Company, Inc.

ISBN 0-7924-5313-1

THE HEARTLAND COMPANION
was prepared and produced by
Tern Enterprise, Inc.
15 West 26th Street
New York, New York 10010

Designer: Judy Morgan
Layout by: Helayne Messing
Photo Editor: Ede Rothaus
Illustrations by Judy L. Morgan

Additional photography: pp. 130–131 © Derek Fell, 18, 83, 86, 87, © Balthazar Korab, 88–89 © Paul T. McMahon/Heartland Images, pp. 98, 106 © William Seitz, 104–105 © Robert Hoebermann

Typeset by: The Interface Group
Color separation by Scantrans Pte. Ltd.
Printed and bound in Singapore by Tien Wah Press Pte. Ltd.

Dedication

To the pioneers who carved homes out of the Heartland wilderness with their blood, sweat, and tears. And to the Native American tribes who lived and worshipped on this land long before the white settlers arrived.

Acknowledgements

Many people go into the making of a book, and this one is no exception. So first I want to thank all the wonderful folks at Heartland companies who sent me catalogs of their unique foods and gifts; especially Sherri Upp at Best Wishes Gift Baskets in Pleasantville, Ohio, for her enthusiasm and research help.

Thanks go to Edith Munro at the Corn Refiner's Association, and Mary Jane Laws at the American Dairy Association, for their help and support early on in the project. Thanks also to Mark Heuer, who helped me perfect the Cincinnati Chili recipe, and to Phil Reekers for his guidance and culinary wit.

Thanks to Jan Riggenbach, garden editor at *Midwest Living* magazine, for her help with the garden chapter, and to Richard Kollath, who devised the twig projects. I also owe a lot to the Ohio Valley Quilter's Association for leading me to Lori Eckert. Lori provided the Ohio Star quilting design and her good natured expertise and attention to detail made her a joy to work with.

No writer can really shine without an editor's support: Thanks to Stephen Williams, who helped keep me on track; to Mary Forsell, who helped fill in the gaps in my knowledge with specific information and make *The Heartland Companion* a better book; and to Ede Rothaus and Judy Morgan who helped make it a beautiful book, as well.

Thanks finally to Michael, whose love and support helped me through the writing process.

CONTENTS

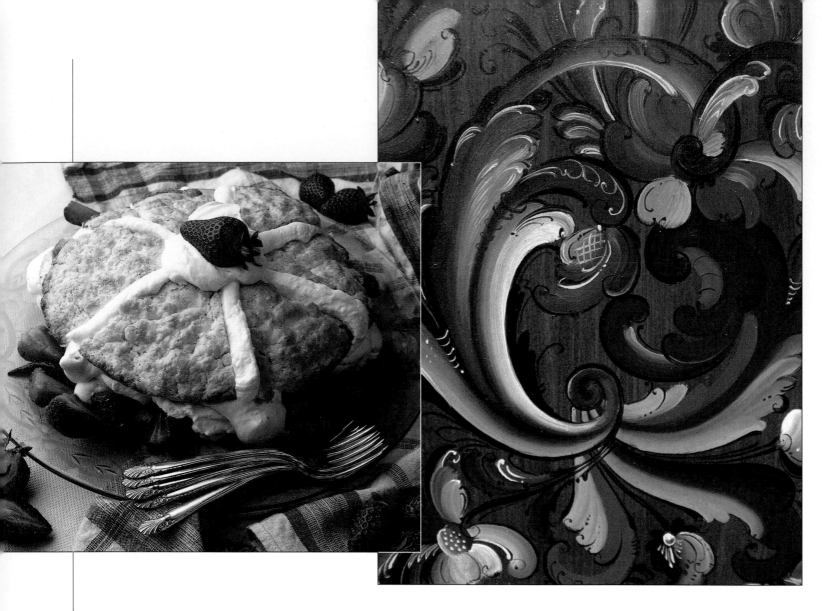

The Midwest is the Heartland of America: a crazy quilt composed of cows and corn-fields, factories and skyscrapers, small towns with big grain elevators and big cities with small apartments, suburbs and shopping malls, farms and forests, freeways and country roads, a checkerboard of green and brown fields with snaking rivers and gently rolling hills. Bounded by the Appalachians to the east, the Rockies to the west, the Ozark Hills to the South, and the Great Lakes to the north, the Midwest includes the states of Ohio, Indiana, Illinois, Michigan, Wisconsin, Minnesota, Missouri, Kansas, Iowa, Nebraska, North Dakota, and South Dakota.

Midwesterners have sturdy pioneer roots. As a vast wilderness inhabited only by Native Americans, fur trappers and traders, the region was the original American frontier. When Horace Greely gave his famous advice, "Go west, young man, and grow up with the country," he wasn't talking about Colorado, he meant the Midwest. And the immigrants created the Breadbasket and the Corn Belt of America. The beauty and open space that farms provide are still an integral part of the Midwest. Farming represents a simple, stable, slow-lane lifestyle. The values that grow out of

this lifestyle—love of nature, love of the earth, and love of nurturing—flavor even the most urban Midwesterners' lives.

The Midwest is a land of contrasts: red barns with silver silos located near elegant condominiums; festivals celebrating everything from pumpkins to performance art; pro sports and pro ballets; wide open prairies and thick forests. Though far from the mountains and the sea, the Heartland is a gigantic manufacturing center and fertile agricultural region; it is also the hub of the nation's transportation system. Thus, it is certainly as important as any other region in North America, with significant impact on the rest of the world. And perhaps more than any other region of the United States, the Heartland symbolizes the challenges and hopes of the American dream and the strength of the American spirit.

This book celebrates the unique heritage of the Heartland. It is your guide to the food, homes, gardens, and crafts of the region. I hope that the Heartland Companion inspires you to further explore this great region.

Beth Franks

HEARTLAND HOMES & INTERIORS

Home in the Heartland isn't just a place, it's a state of mind. Much more than a simple "roof over your head," a house is where family life occurs—where the heart is. In this chapter you're invited home to the Heartland, where a rocking chair, a good book, and a cup of steaming cocoa are waiting by the hearth, and a fire burns cozily to welcome you.

Perhaps as a result of the homesteading tradition, Midwesterners have a reputation for being more concerned with substance than with style. It's true that quality and craftsmanship are paramount; Midwesterners want their homes and everything in them to be solidly put

12

together. They believe a house is meant to be lived in, not just looked at. Although the facade and exterior detailing of a typical Midwestern house may look old-fashioned, inside you're liable to find a state-of-the-art kitchen and bathroom.

But while they are decidedly down-to-earth types, Heartlanders prefer living with things that are pretty as well as practical: Windsor chairs, Oriental rugs, handmade quilts, and needlepoint pillows are just a few of their perennial favorites. They also cherish small architectural details: Porcelain or cut glass doorknobs grace paneled interior doors; simple moldings in oak or maple, without a lot of detail, are characteristic trims.

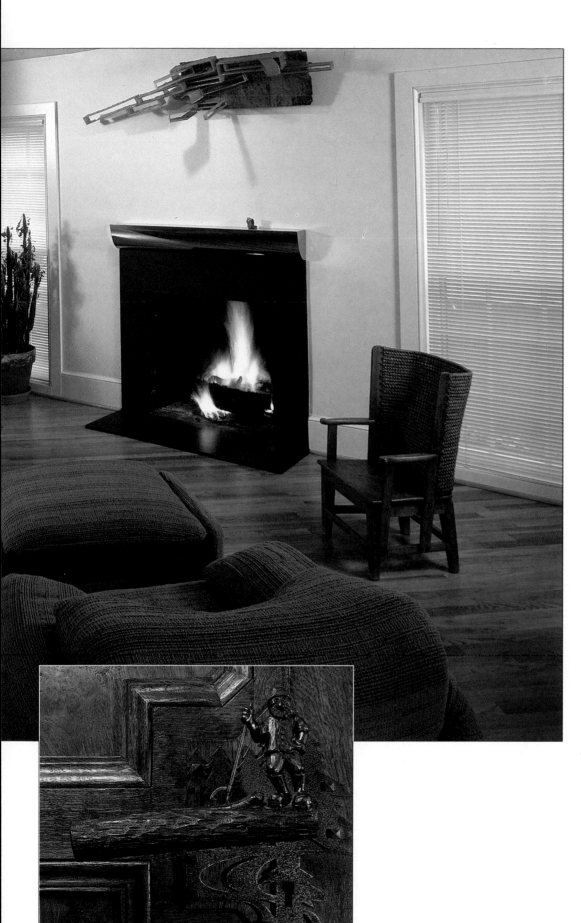

*B*eautiful old homes all over the Heartland are being lovingly restored to their former glory (page 10); one-room schoolhouses like this one (page 12) stand as testimonials to Midwestern pioneer roots. Often eclectic yet unassuming in their tastes, Heartlanders are adept at gracefully combining the old with the new. They appreciate natural materials like wood and stone, and look for ways to incorporate them into a decorating scheme (left). Folk art captures the independent spirit of the Heartland, where creativity is often channeled into making utilitarian objects. Whoever carved this door knob (below) used imagination to solve a practical problem.

13

THE HEART OF THE COUNTRY

It takes a heap o' livin' in a house t' make it home.
—Edgar Guest, Home

When it comes to decorating, Heartlanders love anything country— whether it's American, English, French, or Scandinavian country doesn't matter. Maybe it's because they are do-it-yourselfers, and the country style is easy to put together yourself, with relatively little expense. They're no doubt also attracted by the casual, friendly feeling projected by a country decor and the "undecorated" quality it brings to a room. The style also appeals to Midwesterners' strong sense of family roots.

The country look is typified by natural materials, bright colors, and simple, light-toned wooden furniture. Decors might feature exposed brickwork and beams; plank or parquet floors; stenciled borders; hooked or rag rugs; red gingham, calico, and dainty flowered print textiles; Shaker-style or rustic furniture, large square tables with turned legs; handcrafts (especially baskets, ceramics, and patchwork quilts); and primitive and folk art. Bright, cheery fabrics and finishes are often combined with wood to create an ambiance that's both colorful and friendly.

In recent years, country kitchens have become extremely popular all over the United States. Heartlanders, however, have had country kitchens for years, and are old hands at combining old-fashioned style with the latest conveniences.

Of course, Heartlanders will readily give any room in the house the country treatment, or at least a touch of country. In the bedroom, this might be a four-poster bed with a homespun coverlet; in the living room, a sofa upholstered in fabric inspired by a traditional log cabin quilt pattern; or Shaker chairs in the dining room; a low cedar chest that doubles as seating in the family room; or delicate stenciled borders in the bathroom.

Most likely, Midwesterners are drawn to country style because it evokes the wholesome simplicity of the past. They respect the pioneer spirit of spontaneity and inventiveness embodied in the country style, which made use of whatever materials were available. And they lovingly preserve cultural artifacts, and raise everyday objects to the level of art. Consider, for instance, the newfangled custom of hanging old tools or farm implements on the wall, or using the wall, instead of the bed, to display a quilt.

© Balthazar Korab

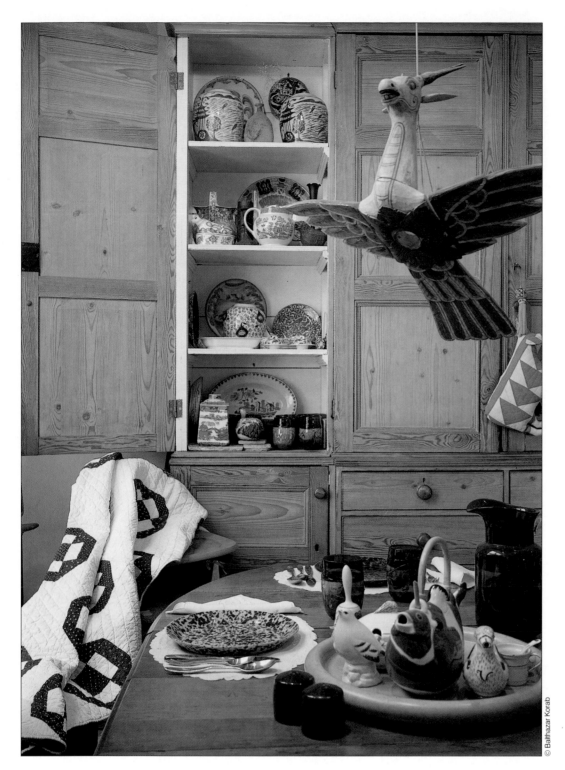

© Balthazar Korab

Many modern Midwestern kitchens are reminiscent of their pioneer predecessors, though rustic charm is often a cover for the latest in streamlined convenience. Evocative of self-sufficiency and natural bounty, these country kitchens are warm and friendly places, truly "the heart of the home" (page 14). Handmade or antique objects are the essence of country style (left). Though these objects might be made of stoneware or blue glass, cloth or wood, their plain, honest utility is cherished by collectors all over the Heartland.

15

*S*tencils (right) range from simple shapes to more elaborate ones, as illustrated here. And although usually associated with country style decors, stenciled motifs are perfectly at home with more formal homes as well. Chippendale furniture (page 17) is identifiable by its cabriole legs and claw-and-ball feet. Often made of mahogany, walnut, or cherry, Chippendale furniture is generously proportioned. It is perfectly at home in formal rooms.

16

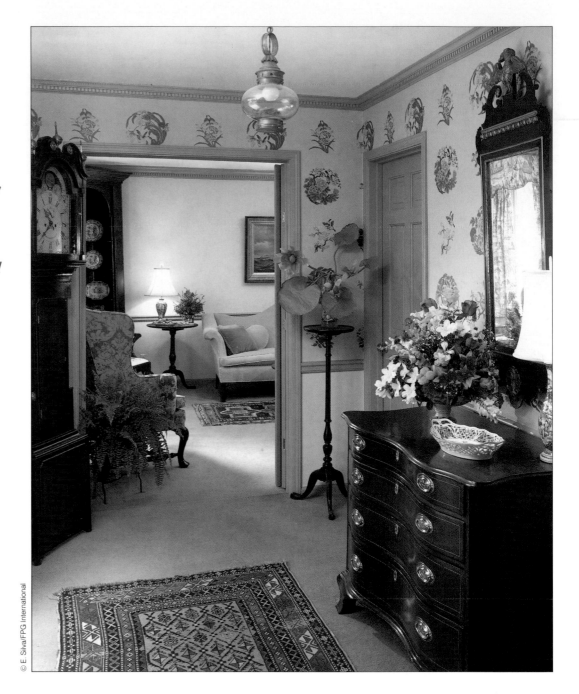

© E. Silva/FPG International

TRADITIONAL DECOR

The traditional style of decorating is another Heartland favorite. Though it's more formal than country, historically, the two styles evolved concurrently. Traditional might be considered an upscale prototype of country: This was how wealthy colonial citizens in cities like New York and Philadelphia were decorating their homes, while rural settlers and pioneers by necessity made sturdier, simplified adaptations of traditional designs. In the olden days, these cruder country pieces were often painted to cover "inferior" woods, as compared to the patina on traditional pieces made of cherry or maple.

Heartlanders, always leery of fads and trends, appreciate that rooms decorated in the traditional manner never go out of style. They especially like to use a traditional decor in their "formal" spaces: living rooms and dining rooms. Designed to last for generations, the graceful shapes of Chippendale, Queen Anne, and Sheraton furniture are light and beautifully balanced. (Fine reproductions are available for those whose taste far exceeds their pocketbook.)

Heartlanders treasure mementos and furnishings that are passed down through the generations, and are good at finding imaginative ways to mix heirlooms with comfortable, contemporary furniture. As individualists, they've been known to design an entire room around a special treasure—a collection of delftware, or an antique deacon's bench and farm table. They like to do things their own way, and they don't care if it's "in" or "out." Some of them also blend casual and formal elements in the same room—hanging a primitive, handpainted picture frame above a Queen Anne sideboard, for instance. Or they'll use country elements in design schemes that aren't in any other way rurally inspired—a twig rocker in a contemporary living room. Ultimately, Heartlanders are too practical to be purists.

*[Home is]
Just a wee cot—the
cricket's chirr—Love
and the smiling face
of her.—James
Whitcomb Riley,*
Ike Walton's
Prayer

17

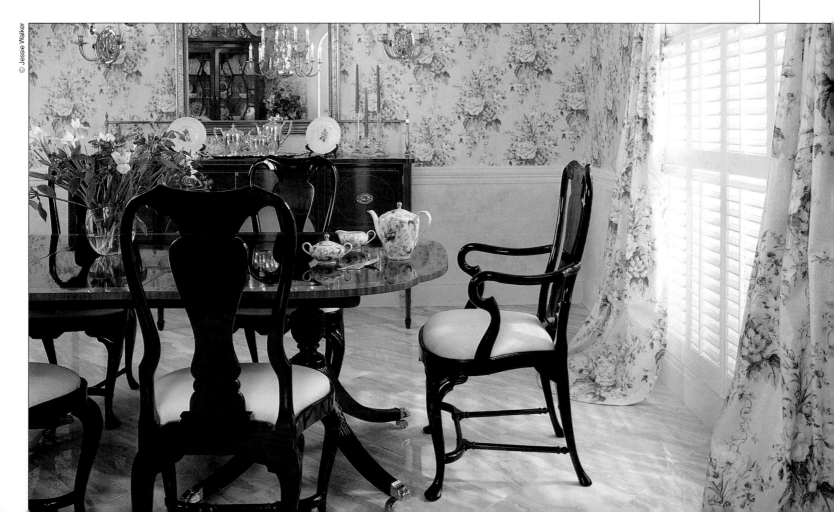

The Victorians adored stained glass—the more ornate, the better. Victorian houses often have glass panels in front doors and the tops of windows executed in stained or beveled glass. But the window on the stairway landing is usually the most fanciful, with everything from landscapes, portraits, Tiffany-style tracery, animals, and birds (like this peacock), rendered in colored glass.

18

The Victorian Revival

In the past few years, some Heartlanders have embraced Victoriana, a romantic treatment especially suited to their formal living and dining spaces as well as their bedrooms. Historically, the Victorian style combines ornate, formal furnishings with sumptuous accessories. The Victorians indulged in a free mix of styles—Rococo, Classical, Elizabethan, Chinese, and Italian Renaissance pieces might inhabit the same room— they loved ornamentation, and were obsessed with details. So although it's a bit rich for the average Heartlander's tastes, Victorian style has a dignified formality that acts as a counterbalance to the casual feel of country.

Victorian decors typically include massive mahogany furniture, upholstered chairs with exposed wood frames, Oriental rugs, marble-topped tables, chandeliers, chaises, stained glass, balloon curtains, painted wicker furniture, bentwood, glass paneled cabinetry, filagree, jardinieres or fern stands, potted palms, porcelain, brass beds, and lots of bric-a-brack. Architecturally, the Victorian emphasis on ornamentation translates into carved bannisters, tall baseboards, thick crown moldings, inside shutters, and "gingerbread" details; walls are always decorated, whether with patterned wallpaper, *trompe l'oeil* scenes, or sponge-painting. Favorite fabrics include lace, silk, velvet, chintz, and damask, in floral patterns, paisleys, or deep solid shades of red or green, often with gold accents.

A well-decorated interior, by Victorian standards, must feature a variety of surfaces. The interior at left has a marble floor in two colors, an ornately carved wooden newel post and stair railing, and a profusion of painted decorations on the walls. The Victorian style touches every surface with ornament. Even ceilings (below) are sometimes very graphic.

19

© Balthazar Korab

© Balthazar Korab

Hallmarks of Midwestern Style

Here are some home design ideas that are important to Heartlanders, and can be found throughout the region:

Many Warm Hearths

Midwestern homes are more likely to have two or more fireplaces than homes in other parts of the country. Native stone is often used to build the fireplaces.

© Balthazar Korab

Porches and Oversize Windows

Heartlanders are always looking for ways to stay in touch with nature. That's why they like houses with screened-in porches or decks; prefer big windows that offer garden views and allow plenty of sunlight in to nurture houseplants.

© William Seitz

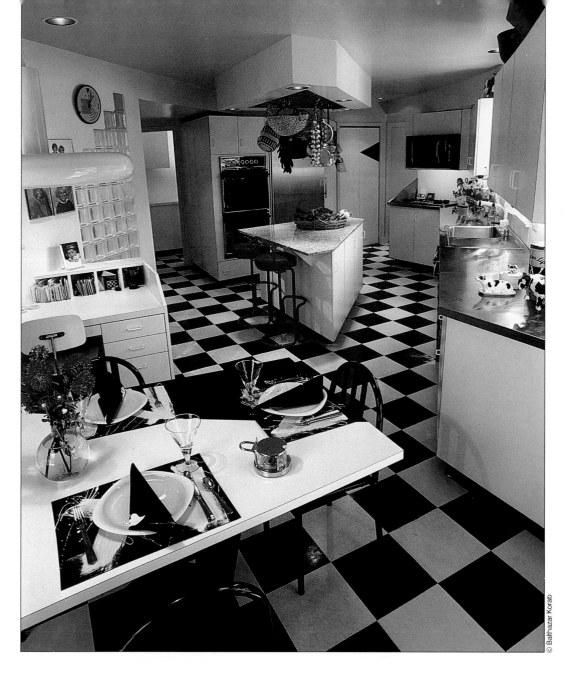

© Balthazar Korab

*T*he hearth (opposite, top) is a focal point of many Heartland rooms today. Heartlanders love an abundance of natural light in their homes. They use skylights, bay windows, and sliding glass doors to minimize the division between indoors and out (opposite, below). The kitchen is often where the family gathers to spend quality time together; maybe that's why big kitchens are de rigueur in the Midwest. When remodeling, people will often take down walls or eliminate closets to achieve the kitchen of their dreams.

21

Rooms Full of Meaning

Heartlanders cherish family heirlooms, passing spinning wheels, hope chests, quilts and other mementos down through the generations, and finding ways to incorporate these treasured old things in modern decors.

Roomy Kitchens

Heartland kitchens are often open to other areas of the house, such as the family room. In addition to cooking and casual dining, Midwestern kitchens are being used for everything from studying to entertaining, and feature things like built-in desks and media centers.

Artists know that the more surfaces a painting has, the more luscious it looks. Glazed walls (right) embody that principle. The semitransparent glaze covers the wall color like a light veil, creating an impression of understated elegance.

Favorite Ways to Brighten a Wall

Heartland interiors are often brightened by an interesting wall design. Here are a few popular techniques.

Glazing

A painted surface is coated with a thinned-down film of oil-based paint (the "glaze"), creating a semitransparent effect. Other special painting techniques sometimes use glazing as an intermediate step, but it stands alone as a subtle way to add elegance and depth.

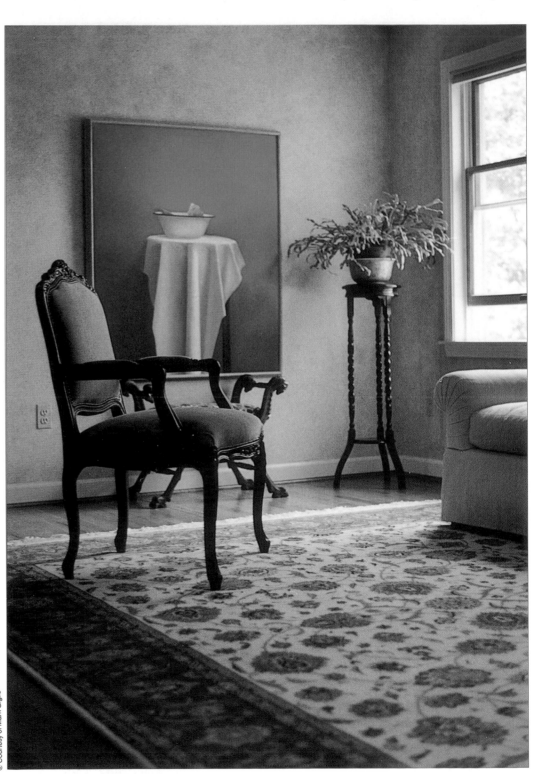

© Courtesy of Mark Giglio

Marbleizing

Arguably the most popular of all special effects with paint, marbleizing instantly brings an old-fashioned touch to any surface. Many Heartland mantels, tabletops, lamp bases, baseboards, trim, moldings, and inset wall panels have been marbleized. By applying paints with brushes, crumpled rags, and feathers, just about any wood surface can be painted to look like marble. This is a more exacting technique than most of the others described here. Colors are blended and streaked, then veined to simulate marble. Colors are usually pale alabasters, pinks, or black for marble, though you'll also find other faux stone surfaces—turquoise and malachite are popular—being painted in darker shades.

Ragging

Using a rag to apply thin, overlapping coats of paint gives walls an interestingly textured patina, evocative of a quaint country cottage.

Rag Rolling

A heavily textured pattern effect used for walls, ceilings, floors, tabletops, and trunks. In this technique, a basecoat of paint is glazed with a darker shade of the same color, then a rag sprinkled with turpentine is rolled over the surface. This pattern will vary according to what kind of rag you use.

DECORATING THE WALL

Heartlanders have always known that one of the easiest ways to enliven a room is to decorate the walls with a pleasing pattern. Since the Victorian era, wallpaper has been the traditional choice in the Midwestern home. In the past, floral patterns and paisleys were favored above all else, and it's possible to re-create that timeless look today by using reproduction Victorian wallpaper. Tea rose and vine patterns are particularly appropriate for Midwestern homes—especially for the old, gable-roof farmhouses that are so prolific in the Ohio countryside.

In the past, people who couldn't afford to wallpaper their homes often opted for stenciling as an inexpensive solution. Itinerant stencil artists wandered through the countryside and offered their services door-to-door. Botanical motifs—including trailing vines and blooming roses—as well as fluid, simple patterns—such as fleur-de-lis—were favored. Stenciling was often done in the living room and in the entryway to the house, continuing up along the stairway. It might also have been found below the ceiling molding, above chair rails, and around windows and doors. Today, your options are limitless, and you can also apply stencils to floors, furniture, and fabric. There are numerous stencil kits and patterns available to create a timeless look in your home.

A subtle yet effective way to draw interest to a room's walls is through decorative woodwork. In the early twentieth century, wood was used prolifically in the Heartland to ornament rooms. At that time, many people—particularly those living in the Chicago area—were collecting furniture and objects inspired by the Arts and Crafts movement. As a result, Midwesterners opted for completely paneled walls, as they provided an understated backdrop for their furnishings. Another traditional option is to add crown molding to the walls. If you want to achieve a more eyecatching look, place wallpaper in the area above the molding.

Sponged walls (right) sport a delicately textured pattern. The natural variations of the sea sponge used to apply the paint create layers of color, which in turn make for a luscious looking surface. Plants and flowers are favorite motifs to stencil because of their natural movement—just as vines grow in nature, the decoration proliferates around a room (page 25, top). Through the careful rendition of tactile and tonal values, this trompe l'oeil mural deceives the eyes, expanding one's perception of space to include an imaginary bookshelf.

24

© William Seitz

Spatterpainting

Thinned paint is applied to the surface by splattering it from a toothbrush. This technique is sometimes used on country-style floors, baseboards, trim, wainscoting, and molding, though it can also look very contemporary. Depending on the colors used and the size and density of the splatters, this style can produce subtle or extreme effects.

Spongeing

This Victorian favorite is easy to do and also looks terrific. A natural sea sponge is dipped in glaze or paint, then gently blotted onto the wall, creating a soft textured look. This technique employs at least two colors; for example, walls might be painted a cream color, then several layers of a dusty rose shade would be sponged on top. It can also be used in combination with other techniques such as spatterpainting and stippling. Spongeing techniques recall the past glory of Midwestern Victorian parlors.

© E.A. McGee/FPG International

Stenciling

In this time-honored technique, paint is applied to the wall through a cut-out pattern. Stenciled designs are often inspired by nature (trailing vines, blooming roses), and show up in both country and Victorian decors. Often these stencils are replicas of old designs; if the house is old, homeowners usually try to choose designs that correspond to the age of the house. Another favorite trick is to coordinate a stencil motif with wallpaper used in the home. Most often appearing below the ceiling molding, above chair rails, and around windows and doors, stencils are also sometimes applied to floors, furniture, and fabric.

Stippling

A textural effect similar to spongeing, stippling is sometimes used in combination with other techniques. In this technique, wet glaze is stroked on a small area, then stippled with a clean, dry paintbrush to create a soft matte finish. Stippling is used on walls, furniture, and accessories in country decors.

Trompe l'oeil

Unlike other painting methods described here, this "fool the eye" technique requires considerable artistic skill to execute. Often used to add architectural features, such as columns, panels, or windows (complete with view), it may also be used to create a texture such as marble or wood grain on a plaster or wood surface.

The Richmond house was built of limestone, and, although it was said in the village to have become run down, had in reality grown more beautiful with every passing year. Already time had begun a little to color the stone, lending a golden richness to its surface and in the evening or on dark days touching the shaded places beneath the eaves with wavering patches of browns and blacks.
—Sherwood Anderson,
Winesburg, Ohio

25

Shelburne Museum, Shelburne, Vermont

THE MIDWESTERN INFLUENCE

The first settlers to the Heartland made their homes out of whatever was at hand—rough wood houses in forested areas, and small, dark houses made of sod on the prairie. But in time the region developed architecturally and many people are surprised at the variety of styles of buildings found in the Heartland.

Some small towns in Iowa and Minnesota are as quaint as the fabled villages of New England. Victorian architectural details on porches and windows clutter entire neighborhoods of houses in the Midwest. Tall trees line the streets, and ornamental gardens fill the frontyards.

The farm towns of plains areas in Kansas and Nebraska are built up with unornamented, forbidding buildings made of limestone and granite quarried locally. These buildings are built to last, and no doubt will be around as long as they are needed.

All of these influences contributed in their way to the explosion of Midwestern architecture in the early part of the twentieth century, when two architects, Frank Lloyd Wright and Louis Sullivan, were developing their craft. While both of these men are known for blasting to bits the stereotype of staid Midwestern conservatism with their modern designs which shook up architectural traditions all over the world, they were still Heartlanders through and through.

© Balthazar Korab

ON MODERN ARCHITECTURE

© Balthazar Korab

One sees rough log houses in rural areas all across the Heartland. Many are in ruins, mute memorials to the settlers who made a home among the Native Americans more than a century ago. Others, like these (top), have been used continuously and carefully tended to over the years. The Victorians loved ornamentation, and they preferred decoration to be grandiose rather than simple. Witness the exaggerated keystone on this Victorian window (bottom).

27

*Hog butcher
for the world,
Tool maker,
stacker of wheat,
Player with railroads
and the nation's
freight handler;
Stormy, husky,
brawling,
City of the
big shoulders.
—Carl Sandburg,*
Chicago

28

© Matthew Kaplan

Form Follows Function

While his contemporaries were reviving classicism, Sullivan looked to living organisms for inspiration in creating his buildings. He designed skyscrapers in the 1890s, with the goal of transforming the mass of steel and stone into "a proud and soaring thing"; his most famous Midwest skyscraper designs include the Wainwright in St. Louis and the Gage Building in Chicago. He also designed the Transportation Building for the world's Columbian Exhibition in Chicago in 1893. Sullivan was the first to say that form follows function, a phrase so often quoted nowadays as to be almost a cliché, but which was revolutionary at the time, as Victorians were pursuing ornamentation as an end in itself. But his uncompromising individualism eventually got him into conflicts with his clients—Chicago's industrial barons—and he spent the last twenty-nine years of his life an architectural outcast.

The Gage building in Chicago (left), and the architectural detail below are typical of Louis Sullivan's architecture.

29

The Prairie School

Frank Lloyd Wright, a Wisconsin native born in 1869, worked as Sullivan's chief apprentice from 1887 to 1893, and Wright acknowledged that he learned a lot from his mentor. During his seventy-year career, Wright designed hundreds of innovative structures, including private residences as well as hotels, schools, office complexes, churches, synagogues, and theaters. Many of these were built in the Heartland, especially in Illinois, Michigan, and Wisconsin.

Wright was the leader and spokesman for a style of architecture known as the Prairie School. The nineteenth century had seen the rise of the Victorian style, when homes were elaborately ornamented—both inside and out—with superfluous decoration, such as gingerbread work and fussy wood carvings. By the time Wright began practicing, new technology had allowed for innovation in home design. It was now possible for precast concrete structures to stand, so interior walls were no longer necessary for holding up a structure.

In the prairie house, the interior space had its own rhythmic flows, not bounded by traditional walls and rigid room divisions. Generously proportioned fireplaces were located in the center of rooms to emphasize the open plan. Wright and other Prairie School architects eliminated moldings and threshold saddles to further reinforce the feeling of unrestricted space. They also limited the types of materials used in the home so that divisions between areas would not be emphasized.

Homes designed in this mode were horizontally oriented and tended to lie close to the ground. Cantilevered overhangs further emphasized this interaction with the ground plane. The house was meant to visually interact with the landscape, rather than contradict it, and echo the lay of the land with its long lines.

31

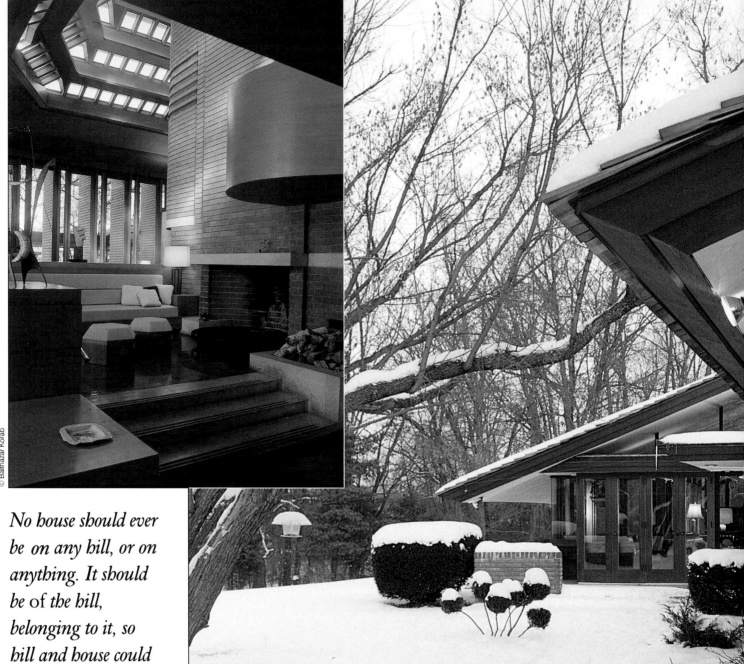

© Balthazar Korab

No house should ever be on any hill, or on anything. It should be of the hill, belonging to it, so hill and house could live together each the happier for the other. —Frank Lloyd Wright

Whenever possible, Wright would orient a building to the south and slightly east, so that it would receive the maximum daylight. He would sometimes alter plans in order to spare existing trees. Numerous second-floor windows were positioned to take in panoramic views. The living area would

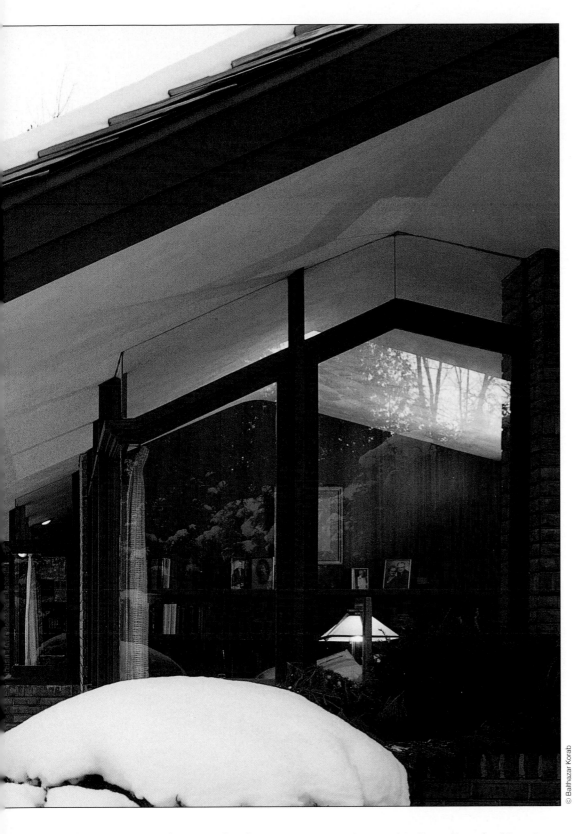

I<i>n 1936, the Johnson Wax Company commissioned Frank Lloyd Wright to design their corporate head-quarters in Racine, Wisconsin (page 32, inset). This private residence in Bloomfield Hills, Michigan, was designed by Frank Lloyd Wright for a local family (page 33).</i>

© Balthazar Korab

often be situated on the upper level to capitalize on these views.

One of the most famous examples of a Wright prairie house is the Frederick Robie House, built in Chicago in 1909. In the 1930s, he went on to design his Usonian (United States-ian) house for families. Based on an L-shaped plan and geared toward informality, the Usonian was designed to be more affordable for the average American. Wright's concept of the open plan extended beyond domestic architecture and still exerts an influence today in the designs of both private homes and corporate buildings.

HEARTLAND FOODS

Midwesterners have hearty appetites and like simple, wholesome foods. Country-style cooking predominates, with an emphasis on high quality, fresh ingredients; cooking "from scratch" never went out of style here. Although city-dwellers in the Heartland have sophisticated palates, and eat everything from fajitas to falafel, typical Heartland meals are direct descendents of farm food. Home-style dishes such as chicken and noodles, meat loaf and mashed potatoes, turkey and dressing, roast chicken and apple fritters, and ham with scalloped potatoes are essential. Although Heartlanders have made some health-conscious diet changes in the past few years, at dinnertime, meat and potatoes still form the backbone of the Midwestern diet.

Until the early 1900s, even breakfast reached epic proportions in the Heartland. Consider a breakfast of pancakes served with bacon fat and molasses, fried eggs, ham, fried potatoes, lots of boiled coffee, bread and jam, fried cornmeal mush, and pie for dessert! But while farm laborers and pioneers might have been able to handle a caloric load like this, life has become more sedentary for most people. And nowadays, in the prevailing climate of concern over cholesterol, this kind of "working man's breakfast" is reserved for very special occasions, such as community get-togethers.

*M*idwestern cooks are much more careful to limit fat and cholesterol in food than they were in the past, but special occasions can be an exception. On holidays, the traditional rich dishes reappear in all their glory (page 34), though margarine and lowfat milk may be substituted for butter and cream. A favorite Midwestern meal is a steak and a baked potato (page 36), especially if the steak is well marbled and tender. Festive Heartland breakfast menus today may be more modest than those of the past, but they are by no means shabby. A typical "big breakfast" (left) features scrambled eggs, sausage or bacon, fried potatoes, toast, and coffee.

FRONTIER COOKING IN THE HEARTLAND

No matter what conditions, Dyspeptic come to feaze, The best of all physicians Is apple pie and cheese!—Eugene Field, Apple Pie and Cheese

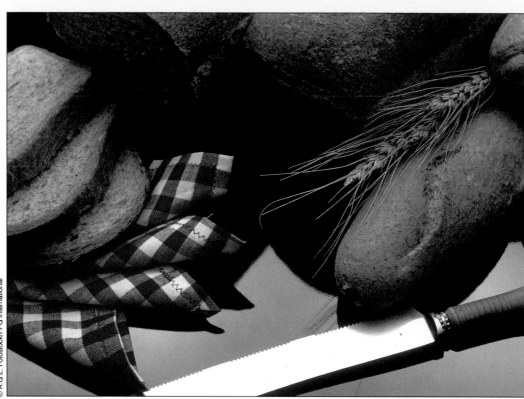

© A.G.E. Fotostock/FPG International

The Heartland's simple brand of country cooking has its roots in the pioneer heritage. One hundred and fifty years ago, as the first European settlers in the Midwest struggled to establish a toehold in the wilderness, beans were a staple of the diet. Dried beans kept well, traveled well, were high in protein and calories, and not only offered variety—garbanzos, kidneys, pintos, navies, lentils, and black-eyed peas, to name a few—but could be prepared with whatever vegetables or meat happened to be available.

Root vegetables like potatoes, parsnips, and turnips also stored well, as did apples, and to a lesser extent, cabbage. Women devised lots of clever ways to prepare meals from this rather limited larder. Apples, for instance, might be made into apple butter or apple sauce, apple fritters or apple fraces (thin slices of apple dipped in sweet batter, then fried), apple dumplings or apple pie, apple cider, or just plain old dried

apples. Cabbage could be made into slaw, or shredded and then baked, or cooked with beef.

Stews were used to stretch meat (or use up less desirable cuts), and soups made great rib-sticking sustenance for cold weather. Heartland cooks these days have lots of traditional recipes for both, including beef stew, nine-bean soup, Mulligan stew with venison or lean beef, corn chowder, tomato soup, potato soup, cream of celery or asparagus soup, chicken noodle soup, and pea soup.

And what makes a better complement to a hearty bowl of soup than a thick slice of homemade bread? Crusty wheat bread, herb and nut bread, rye bread, sweet buttermilk batter bread, corn bread dripping with butter, or egg skillet bread—the Heartland baker has a long tradition of improvisational skill, with the ability to make something delicious out of whatever ingredients are at hand.

© Steven Mark Needham/Envision

There's nothing cozier than the smell of freshly baked bread (page 38). The Heartland is as all-American as apple pie; succulent versions of the national dessert are made daily in kitchens across the region. The crust must be light and flaky, the apple filling thick with juice and delicately flavored with cinnamon, though the pie may be topped with either crust or streusel. Apple pie is often served with vanilla ice cream, though some folks prefer their pie topped with cheddar cheese.

39

© Jeanetta Ho

*W*ild rice (right)
has grown in
the lakes and rivers
of Minnesota and
Wisconsin for centuries.
It was so important to
the Native Americans
that the late summer
moon was called
"Menominikegississ"—
the rice making moon.
They used wild rice as
medicine, as decoration
for clothing, for food,
and in barter. Often,
wild rice is still
harvested in the
traditional way today,
by two people in a
canoe. Heartland
cooks are not afraid to
experiment, combining
traditional ingredients
in unusual ways.
Consider this delight-
fully unexpected
mixture: a wild rice
salad with Greek olives
and prunes (page 41).

Wild Foods

Despite civilization's continual encroachment on the wilderness, the Heartland remains a hunting and fishing paradise. Many of the same animals hunted by the pioneers are still prized today, including deer, pheasant, duck, fish, frogs, rabbits, and even squirrels, woodchucks, and possums for the real backwood types. The hunting tradition dates back to pioneer days, when if you wanted meat, you had to kill it yourself —if you could find it. Maybe that's why to this day a meal of wild game retains a certain air of celebration. Other wild foods—wild rice and morels, for instance—make an appropriate side dish.

With its distinctive nutty flavor, wild rice complements just about any hunter's feast—or any meal, for that matter. Known to the Sioux and Chippewa Indians as "menomin" or "good grain," wild rice is actually not rice at all, but a rare aquatic grass. In late August, the Native Americans of Minnesota would harvest the precious grain by bending the stalks over their birch-bark canoes and flailing the plants with cedar sticks to shake the ripe grains loose. Although the great rice beds are mostly gone now, Native Americans still harvest wild rice in Minnesota and Wisconsin. This luxury food is now grown commercially in California, driving down profits for Native American harvesters, but making the grain more affordable.

Wild mushrooms taste great with wild rice. Fortunately, the Heartland is a wild mushroom forager's paradise and

*M*orel mushrooms are rare; you may need sharp eyesight to spot them. Once discovered, they must be carefully cleaned—either rinsed several times or gently rubbed with a brush. Dark brown to black caps are more prized than lighter morels. Purists insist that morels be braised in butter alone, though others prepare them in a sauce thickened with fresh cream or flavored with wine.

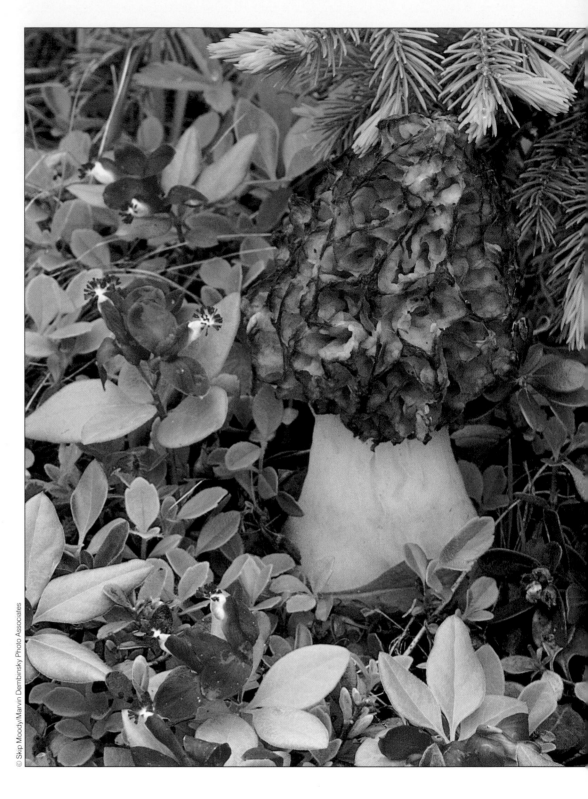

© Skip Moody/Marvin Dembinsky Photo Associates

abounds with such popular types as morels and puffballs. Easy to identify by their conical, pitted caps, morels are prized as one of the finest edible mushrooms. They are found May through September in apple orchards, as well as in maple or beech woods.

Puffballs thrive from August to October in deep woods, as well as in the cultivated and waste lands at the edges of fields and meadows, on rotten logs, and in piles of leaves. Connected to the ground by a sort of cord, puffballs usu-

ally grow to 8 to 15 inches in diameter.

Before you go hunting and gathering, learn to identify wild mushrooms, because some wild mushrooms and puffballs are deadly poisonous. If you're a beginner, it's a good idea to invest in a field guide, and to go hunting with someone experienced until you know what you are doing. False morels look vaguely like the real thing, but they are irregular and contorted; they lack the distinct pitted appearance of morels, and appear wrinkled instead.

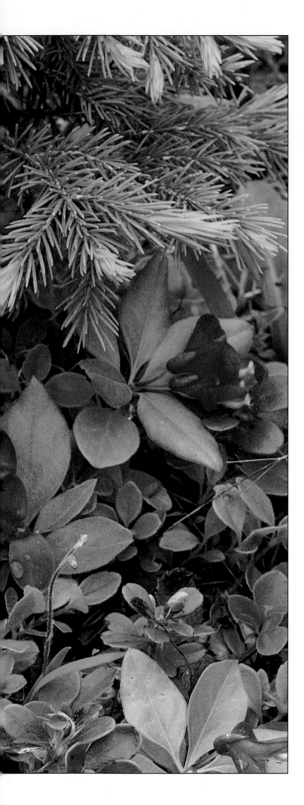

This slogan, from a 1903 advertisement for Kellogg's Corn Flakes, is significant to the Heartland, because dry breakfast cereal was invented in Battle Creek, Michigan. John Kellogg and his brother W.K. ran a sanitarium in Battle Creek in accordance with the teachings of the Seventh Day Adventists and their own theory of "Biologic Living." The program was built around proper diet, not drugs. Patients, however, complained that the sanitarium's food was boring; some even left before their treatment was finished because the food was so bad. So sometime around 1880, the Kellogg brothers set up a small laboratory in the kitchen, hoping to develop vegetarian foods that would be both digestible and flavorful.

In one series of experiments they ran boiled wheat dough through rollers to create thin sheets. They then toasted the sheets and ground them into meal. The result, as you can imagine, was less then spectacular. But one day in 1884, both John and W.K. were suddenly called away from the lab, and they had to leave a batch of boiled wheat exposed to the air. When they returned more than twenty-four hours later the wheat had started to mold, but as an experiment, they put it through the rollers anyway. To their delight, instead of the usual sheet of wheat, many light, thin flakes, one for each wheat berry, came tumbling off the rollers. They baked the flakes, which came out crisp and tasty, aside from the slight moldiness, and thus the first flaked cereal, Granose, was born.

Using the same process, they developed corn flakes in 1898. These original corn flakes were made from the whole corn kernel, but weren't as popular as wheat flakes. Then W.K. tried making flakes using only the grit, or heart of the corn, adding a little malt for flavor. The result was tastier. Thus the Kellogg's Corn Flakes brand was born.

More than thirty other cereal companies sprang up in and around Battle Creek, a city of less than 30,000, in imitation of the Kelloggs' success. One company was set up by a former patient at the sanitarium, C.W. Post. None of the other companies manufactured corn cereal, however, and W.K. was convinced that corn flakes would become the most popular ready-to-eat cereal of all time. To avoid confusion with his competitors' products, W.K.'s signature was printed on the Corn Flakes package along with the words, "The original bears this signature."

Puffballs must be cut open and checked. Never eat a puffball that is not evenly textured and white as a marshmallow throughout—avoid yellow or purple mushrooms, those that are unevenly colored, and those with an apparent stem on the inside.

Morels are delicious sautéed in butter and served on toast. Puffballs are good in salads or they can be fried like morels. Unlike morels, which lose the better half of their flavor if not eaten fresh, puffballs can be dried.

*B*read comes in many sizes and shapes in the Heartland, from loaves and sticks to rounds and stuffed pies. Whether they're called pasties, calzones, or runzas, these stuffed pies are standard fare in several ethnic cuisines—probably because they're delicious, filling, and easy to eat.

44

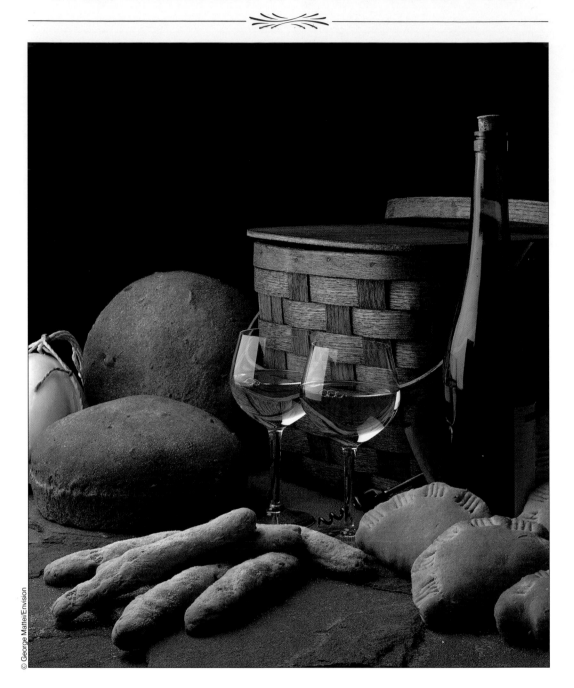

© George Mattei/Envision

Throughout the nineteenth century, many immigrants came directly to the Heartland from Europe, where word had spread of the fertile land available for the taking. Thus recipes from Scandinavia, Germany, Poland, Italy, Ireland, England, Scotland, and France found their way into Heartland cuisine. The following are examples of some of the ethnic threads in the Heartland's heritage.

With the Germans came meat dishes like *sauerbraten* (pickled beef), *hasenpfeffer* (rabbit stew cooked with gingersnaps and port), *fleisch rolle den* (literally,

"roll the meat"), *gemuse* (a meat and vegetable stew), and *wiener schnitzel* (breaded veal cutlet). German cooks concocted a variety of dumplings— *spaetzle* (egg dumplings), *kartoffelklosse* (potato dumplings), *zwetschken knodel* (plum dumplings), and *butterklosse* (butter dumplings)—as well as *pfannkuchen* (pancakes). Rye bread, sauerkraut, sweet and sour cabbage, and hot potato salad were standard side dishes. For dessert there was strudel with nuts or apple, *bund kuchen* (pound cake), *lebkuchen* (honey cake), *springerle* (anise cookies), and *kuechles* (little fried cakes).

Germans also excelled at making a variety of sausages, or *wurst*, including weiners (mildly seasoned pork), *mettwursts* (more highly seasoned), and *bratwurst* (from veal). Finally, with their thirst for beer, Germans brewed their own brands of lager and pilsner, and introduced the *bier garten* to this country.

Scandinavians founded dozens of communities in the Midwest. Danes settled in western Iowa, Swedes in Kansas and northern Illinois, and Norwegians throughout Minnesota. And Scandinavians contributed many foods to the Heartland heritage, including Swedish meatballs, *lefse* (large, thin, potato pancakes, buttered and folded), stuffed cabbage rolls, *lutefisk* (cured, boiled fish), pickled herring, *pult* (ham-stuffed grated potato dumplings), *hootsla* (egg skillet bread), Havarti cheese, rice pudding, *flatbrod* (flatbread), Danish *kringle* (a flat oval pastry, reputedly borrowed from the Austrians), *nisa bread* (a Finnish rye bread spiced with cardamon), Swedish *julekage* (fruit bread and almond twists), and *drommar* ("dreams"), a heavenly cookie. The Dutch settled in Michigan, Iowa, Illinois, Wisconsin, and Minnesota and brought recipes for *gevulde karbonade* (pork chop with apple dressing), spiced beef, *erwtensoep* (pea soup), *kalfslapjes* (sautéed veal), and apple bread.

Numerous other groups contributed their unique fare: Irish soda bread, Polish kielbasa, African-American greens, Italian frittata, and Chinese chow mein, to name a few. Many of the recipes from different countries were in fact different versions of the same thing. As the editors of the *Minnesota Heritage Cookbook: Hand-me-down Recipes* write in their foreword: "As recipes started coming in from all over the state, we quickly realized that we are all brothers and sisters under the dough; the spaetzle, the won ton, the kreplach, the pierogi and the piroshki unite us all." We might add the *gnocchi* and the pasty, too.

Festivals are held every year throughout the Heartland to celebrate the various ethnic heritages. Oktoberfests are celebrated all over the Heartland from September through October; Dutch festivals are held at any time of year in Michigan, Iowa, Minnesota, and Wisconsin; Scandinavian festivals are held May through October in northern parts of the region, and the list goes on. State tourism offices as well as regional magazines can keep you informed.

Good Plain Fare

Amish and Mennonite women are known to be uncommonly good cooks. The Heartland's culinary heritage owes a lot to these "plain people," who began settling in Indiana, Ohio, and Kansas as early as the 1830s. In *Cooking From Quilt Country: Hearty Recipes From Amish and Mennonite Kitchens*, Marcia Adams has collected almost two hundred recipes from the women of northern Indiana, which has the third largest Amish-Mennonite population in the United States. In the process of collecting the recipes, Ms. Adams noticed that there are three distinct regional food communities (and styles of cooking), including German, Swiss, and Alsatian (from the Alsace-Lorraine region of France). And none of these styles is quite the same as the Pennsylvania Dutch cuisine of Lancaster County, Pennsylvania.

Then your apples all is gathered, and the ones a feller keeps Is poured around the cellar-floor in red and yeller heaps; And your cider-makin's over, and your wimmern-folks is through With their mince and apple butter, and theyr souse and saussage,too!…
—*James Whitcomb Riley,* When the Frost is on the Punkin

45

Aunt Francis's Lebkucken

The original recipe for these Mennonite "honey cakes" specified that you should "let the dough sit for two or three days, to ripen," but overnight in the refrigerator is a safer bet. These cookies will keep for up to six months in a tightly sealed tin.

1 pound honey

2 cups light brown sugar

1/4 cup water

5 1/2 cups unbleached flour

1/2 teaspoon baking soda

1/4 teaspoon cloves

1/4 teaspoon cinnamon

1/2 pound blanched almonds

1/4 pound citron

1/4 pound candied orange rind

2 eggs

for the transparent icing

1 cup confectioner's sugar

5 teaspoons boiling water

1/4 cup lemon juice

1 teaspoon vanilla

Heat honey, brown sugar, and water to boiling. Reduce heat and simmer for 5 minutes. Remove from heat, allow to cool. Sift together flour, soda, and spices. Slowly stir this dry mixture into the honey, once it has cooled. Add eggs, almonds, citron, and orange peel. Work into a loaf, and allow to "age" overnight in the refrigerator in a covered crock.

The next day, remove the dough from the refrigerator and allow it to reach room temperature. Preheat oven to 350 degrees. Then work it again lightly, adding more flour if necessary. Roll dough out to 1/4" thickness, then cut into 1-by-3-inch pieces. Bake on greased cookie sheets for 15 minutes.

Combine transparent icing ingredients and mix until smooth. Spread on cookies while they are still warm.

Makes 8 dozen cookies

Zwiebelkuchen

Don't let the onions scare you. This traditional Mennonite onion cake is a delicious quichelike dish that's great as an appetizer, a meal, or a snack. It's particularly good with a fresh salad and Rhine wine.

3 to 4 slices bacon

2 cups chopped onions

2 teaspoons caraway seeds

1 1/2 teaspoons flour

1/2 cup half-and-half (milk may be substituted)

3 eggs, beaten

1/3 cup grated Monterey Jack cheese

*9-inch pie pastry
(frozen, or use recipe that follows)*

Preheat oven to 375 degrees. Fry the bacon and then dice it. Drain most of the fat from the pan and sauté the onions. When the onions are very soft and translucent, add caraway seeds. Stir in flour, then slowly add half-and-half. Remove from heat. Add a little of the mixture to the beaten eggs, then combine the two. Sprinkle grated cheese in the bottom on the pie pastry, then spoon the egg mixture lightly on top. Bake in a 375 degree oven for 35 to 40 minutes, or until pastry is golden and filling is firm.

Serves 6, or 8 to 10 as appetizers

Pastry

(This recipe makes two 9-inch pie crusts. Use one and freeze the other to make this another time.)

2 cups flour

1 teaspoon salt

2/3 cup butter or shortening

4 teaspoons water

Combine flour and salt. Cut in butter with pastry blender. Sprinkle with water, 1 teaspoon at a time, mixing with fork. Gather dough together with fingers until it cleans bowl. Press into ball, roll out.

Divide in half; on a lightly floured board, roll each half into a larger circle. Working lightly and quickly, roll to 1/8-inch thickness and place in pie pan. Avoid overhandling dough.

To freeze the extra piecrust, roll out the dough and place it in a pie pan. Then put the pan in a large Ziplock bag, with as little air as possible, and put it in the freezer.

Makes one pie and one extra crust

Irish Soda Bread

This sweet and crumbly quick bread was introduced to the Heartland by the first Irish immigrants. It is great for breakfast, brunch, or snacks. Wrapped in aluminum foil and tied with a festive ribbon, the distinctive round loaves also make great gifts.

4 cups sifted flour

1 teaspoon salt

1 teaspoon baking soda

1 cup sugar

3/4 cup butter

1 cup raisins

1 tablespoon caraway seeds

1 1/2 cups buttermilk

Preheat the oven to 350 degrees.

Sift dry ingredients together. Add butter, cut it in with a pastry blender or fork. Add raisins and caraway; gradually add buttermilk. Turn dough on a floured board; work for one minute. Add a little more flour if necessary, but dough should remain somewhat sticky. Cut the dough in half; form into two balls. Put on greased baking sheet and make a bold impression of a cross in the top of each ball. (This not only has the practical effect of preventing the bread from cracking as it bakes, but also acts as a religious invocation.) Brush the top with buttermilk, then bake until done, about one hour.

Makes two loaves

HEARTLAND SPECIALTIES

Over the years, certain foods have been associated with specific places in the Midwest. For example, North Dakota leads the nation in raising sunflowers, and cooks there have created everything from sunflower pies—as sinfully rich as pecan pie—to sunflower milk shakes. The following is by no means a complete list of Heartland specialties, but is a representative sampling.

Pasties and Runzas

In Michigan's Upper Peninsula, the signature food is the pasty (pronounced PAH-stee or PAST-ee): a hefty little meat-and-potato pie surrounded by a dark, flaky round crust. Imported by Cornish settlers who came to work in the Upper Peninsula's iron mines in the mid-nineteenth century, the pasty was a perfect miner's lunch—it fit in a pocket, could be warmed up on the end of a shovel, and required no cutlery to eat. When Finnish miners settled in the area they also began making pastys, though they changed the filling slightly. Thus while the Cornish pasty was filled with cubes of steak, the Finnish version was stuffed with a peppery combination of beef, pork, and potatoes, with red onion and carrots or rutabaga.

Cincinnati Chili

Created by the Greek immigrants who settled in Cincinnati, this unique blend of spices, beans, onions, and cheese atop a pile of spaghetti noodles must be tasted to be believed. In 1922, brothers Tom and John Kiradjieff opened a chili parlor next to the Empress Burlesque Theater on Vine Street. Empress Chili was followed by Skyline Chili in 1949 and Gold Star in 1965, and pretty soon Cincinnati began calling itself "The Chili Capital of the World." There are hundreds of chili parlors in the city, aforementioned chains as well as mom-and-pop operations, and all serve the special flavorful concoction known as Cincinnati chili. Family recipes are carefully guarded, but special ingredients are said to include chocolate and cinnamon.

Italian Beef

From the streets of Chicago comes the Italian beef sandwich, made of juicy roast beef flavored with garlic, sliced razor thin, garnished with roasted peppers or giardiniera, and served on a big crusty roll. (Giardiniera is a spicy Italian marinated pepper relish of cauliflower, red bell peppers, olives, celery, carrots, and pepperoncini.) A "half-and-half," or "combo," includes a charcoal-grilled Italian sausage with the pile of beef, and the whole thing is smothered with roasted sweet peppers.

Beef

Where's the beef? All over the Midwest. Kansas City, Missouri, is famous for its sirloin strip steak. Guaranteed to be delicious, no matter what the cut, sirloin is served all across town at reasonable prices. Another Kansas City beef specialty is barbequed brisket and ribs.

In Iowa, diners prize juicy T-bone steaks with haystack potatoes (hash browns), Iowa pea salad—a mixture of peas, cheese, onion, celery, and mayonnaise—and enormous cinnamon rolls.

In Siouxland—the area surrounding Sioux City, Iowa, that also includes parts of Nebraska and South Dakota—you'll find something called a loose-meats sandwich. These sandwiches, also called taverns, Charlie Boys, Tastees, and Maid-Rites, consist of spicy hamburger that's fried to a crumble, as if for a sauce. Or as Jane and Michael Stern describe it in their book *Real American Food:* "Like a sloppy joe, but without the slop." The meat is served on a hamburger bun.

The Sterns also report that fried calf brain sandwiches are a St. Louis specialty, served in taverns all across town; there's even an annual brain cookoff. The brains are dipped in beer batter, then fried and served on rye with pickles and mustard. The best sandwiches are made of an intact half brain rather than with ground up meat.

From Kansas to the Dakotas, fields of sunflowers stretch as far as the eye can see. Sunflowers tolerate heat and drought as long as they get plenty of sunlight; the heads of mature prairie flowers follow the sun as the day passes.

51

Second City Pizzas

The pizza wars in Chicago have produced everything from pizza pot pie to flaming pizza. In 1947 the owners of Uno's restaurant in Chicago invented deep-dish pizza—a pan pizza with an extra-thick crust topped with gourmet ingredients that range from Italian sausage to crabmeat. Then in 1973, Giordano's of Chicago introduced stuffed pizza—a twin crusted deep-dish pizza packed with meats and cheeses, the top crust brushed with a tomato sauce and dusted with Parmesan, Romano, and Italian spice. A restaurant called Edwardo's took pizza to the outer limits in Chicago, with its pizza souffle.

Pork Tenderloin

Illinois and Iowa are well known for producing pork, and lunch in these states often consists of a tenderloin sandwich. (These days, hog farmers are quick to point out that because of genetic improvements, pork is fifteen percent less fatty than it was thirty years ago, and compares favorably with beef, dark turkey meat, and chicken in cholesterol count.) Pounded to tenderness, then fried to a crisp, the tenderloin cutlet is served on a hamburger bun. A variation is the sandy mash, half a sandwich served with mashed potatoes and gravy.

Lake Superior Whitefish

It must be tasted to be believed— slightly dry, but light and flaky, a tender, delicately flavored fish completely devoid of "fishiness." A meal of fresh fish from the Great Lakes is especially good when served with a salad of spinach and bacon, hot poppy seed rolls, and a carrot and raisin slaw.

*F*resh whitefish is a delicacy not only in the region, but nationally. Served with broccoli and roasted potatoes, whitefish makes a legendary meal.

54

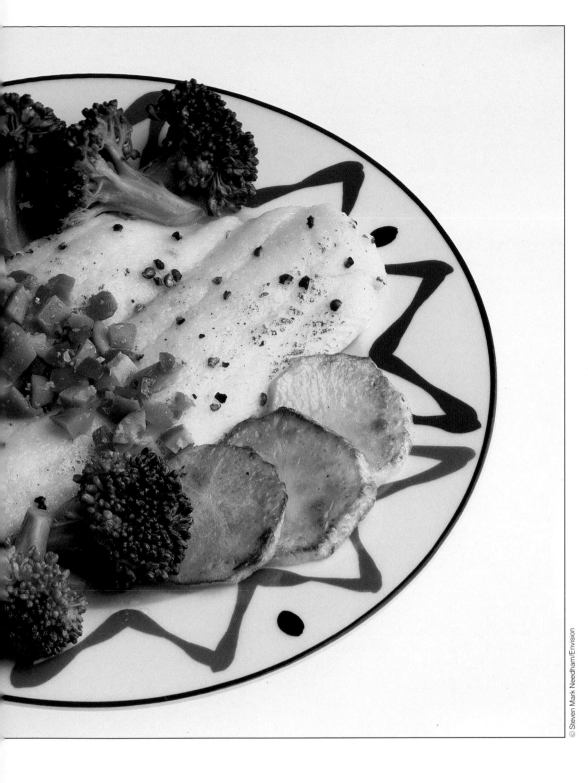

If this is coffee, please bring me a cup of tea, but on the other hand, if this is tea, please bring me a cup of coffee.
—*Abraham Lincoln*

55

Savory Meat Loaf

Meat loaf is an old standby in Heartland kitchens. Unassuming yet delicious, it makes a stick-to-your-ribs meal when served with a baked potato, salad, and green beans. Leftovers turn up in lunch boxes as meatloaf sandwiches.

1 cup tomato juice

3/4 cup oatmeal, uncooked

1 egg, beaten

1/2 cup chopped onion

1 teaspoon salt

1 teaspoon parsley

1/2 teaspoon savory

1/4 teaspoon pepper

1 clove garlic, pressed

1 teaspoon Worcestershire sauce

1 1/2 pounds lean ground beef

Preheat oven to 350 degrees.
   Mix together all ingredients except ground beef, stirring well. Add ground beef and mix thoroughly. Press into 8-by-4-inch loaf pan. Bake one hour. Allow to cool in pan for at least 5 minutes before slicing.

Serves 6

Spicy Molasses Cookies

These easy-to-make cookies are just the thing to warm you up on a snowy winter day.

3/4 cup butter or margarine

1 cup brown sugar

1 egg

1/4 cup molasses

2 1/2 cups flour

2 teaspoons soda

1/2 teaspoon salt

1 teaspoon ginger

1 teaspoon cinnamon

1 teaspoon cloves

Preheat oven to 375 degrees.
   Blend butter, sugar, egg, and molasses until smooth and creamy. Sift in dry ingredients and stir until blended. Chill for 2 hours, then shape the dough into little balls the size of walnuts. Place on greased cookie sheets and bake for 12 minutes.

Makes 3 dozen cookies

Popovers

These light, airy biscuits expand to twice their original size, and are popular at Heartland breakfasts and brunches. They mix up quickly. But be sure to allow enough time for baking.

2 eggs, beaten

1 cup milk

1 cup flour

1/2 teaspoon salt

Preheat oven to 425 degrees.

Mix all ingredients until smooth. Pour into greased muffin tins and bake for 40 minutes.

Makes 6 popovers

Turkey Wild Rice Casserole

(Reprinted with permission of Swift-Eckrich, Inc.)

Wild foods are popular in the Heartland, and this recipe makes elegant use of wild rice and turkey. You can substitute wild mushrooms for store-bought.

6 ounces long grain and wild rice mix

$^3/_4$ pound cooked breast of turkey, cut into $^1/_2$-inch cubes (about 2 cups)

5 large mushrooms, sliced and sautéed in butter (or one 2$^1/_2$ ounce jar of mushrooms, drained)

$^1/_2$ cup coarsely shredded carrot

$^1/_2$ cup finely chopped broccoli

1 cup shredded Swiss cheese, divided into $^1/_2$ cup portions

$^3/_4$ cup half-and-half (or milk, if you prefer)

2 tablespoons sherry

$^1/_4$ teaspoon ground black pepper

3 tablespoons Parmesan cheese

2 tablespoons sliced green onions

Preheat oven to 350 degrees. Prepare rice according to package directions. Combine rice, turkey, mushrooms, carrot, broccoli, and $^1/_2$ cup Swiss cheese in a 2-quart baking dish. Combine half-and-half, sherry, and pepper. Fold into turkey mixture. Cover with remaining Swiss cheese. Sprinkle with Parmesan cheese. Bake 30 to 40 minutes, or until hot and bubbly. Top with green onions and serve.

Serves 5 to 6

Grandma Huttenbauer's Sugar Cookies

This is a wonderful old family recipe for traditional, and much-loved cookies.

1 cup butter

2 cups granulated sugar, sifted

3 eggs, well beaten

1 teaspoon vanilla

4 cups flour

1 teaspoon baking powder

2 teaspoons cinnamon

Preheat oven to 375 degrees.

Beat butter and 1$^3/_4$ cups of the sugar in a large bowl until fluffy. Add eggs and vanilla and continue beating as you gradually add dry ingredients, except cinnamon. (For easier handling, refrigerate the dough for several hours or overnight.) Roll out $^1/_3$ of dough at a time on a lightly floured surface, to about $^3/_8$-inch thickness—very thin. Cut into rectangles about 1$^1/_2$ by 4 inches; place on greased cookie sheets. Run the tines of a fork down the center of each cookie to make indentations. Combine the remaining sugar with the cinnamon and sprinkle this over the cookies. Bake for ten minutes, or until just light brown; cool on a rack.

Makes 4 dozen cookies

Herb Nut Bread

Substantial and slightly sweet, this Heartland bread is so good you may be tempted to make an entire meal out of it.

¹/₂ to ³/₄ cup honey

3 cups warm water

3 heaping tablespoons active dry yeast

3 tablespoons onion

3 cloves garlic

1 teaspoon butter

1 teaspoon salt

3 tablespoons dill weed

3 tablespoons parsley

3 tablespoons poppy seed

4¹/₂ cups unbleached flour

4¹/₂ cups whole wheat flour

1 egg

³/₄ cup olive oil

1 cup oats

1 cup sunflower seeds

¹/₂ cup sesame seeds

Mix the honey and warm water; add yeast. (Active dry yeast works best in water with temperatures between 105 and 115 degrees.) Set mixture aside.

Sauté the onion and garlic in butter. Add salt, dill, parsley, and poppy seed to the sauté pan, then mix into the honey-yeast water. Mix the two types of flour together. Next, add 3 to 5 cups flour mixture, egg, oil, oats, sunflower seeds, and sesame seeds.

Add more flour; turn onto a floured board and knead until dough is smooth and elastic, adding more flour if necessary to manage dough. Shape dough into a large ball, place in a greased bowl, cover and let rise about an hour, or until doubled in size. Punch down; let rise again for about 30 minutes, or until almost doubled in bulk.

Preheat oven to 350 degrees. Shape dough into loaves; place in oiled pans, cover, and let rise 15 minutes. Oil top and bake about 30 minutes.

Makes 2 loaves.

When God gives hard bread He gives sharp teeth.
—German proverb

58

Cincinnati Chili

To be truly authentic, Cincinnati chili must be served on top of spaghetti with a side of oyster crackers. For a "3-way," top the spaghetti and chili with cheese; a "4-way" includes onions underneath the cheese; and the "5-way" also has beans. All the local chili parlors guard their recipes closely, but this version uncovers some of the secrets.

2 pounds lean ground beef

1 quart cold water

2 large onions, chopped

3 cloves garlic, crushed

one 6-ounce can tomato paste

1 tablespoon vinegar

1 tablespoon unsweetened cocoa

1 tablespoon chili powder

2 teaspoons cumin

2 bay leaves

1 teaspoon cayenne pepper

1 teaspoon cinnamon

$^1/_2$ teaspoon allspice

3 drops Tabasco sauce

$^1/_2$ teaspoon crushed red pepper (optional)

Serve with:

1 pound cooked spaghetti

1 pound cheddar cheese, grated

one 16-ounce can kidney beans (optional)

1 onion, finely chopped (optional)

oyster crackers (side dish)

Crumble raw meat into water. Add remaining ingredients, with the exception of spaghetti, cheese, beans, onion, and crackers. Cover and simmer for 3 hours or more, stirring occasionally. Serve over spaghetti, topped with cheese; for additional flavor, add hot kidney beans and raw onions as described above for a 4- or 5-way. Supply a bottle of Tabasco on the side for hot-food aficionados.

Serves 6 to 8

Red Cabbage Salad

This marinated salad adds color and crunch to any meal, and makes an exotic substitute for cole slaw. The sesame oil gives it a nutty taste, and the mustard gives it tang.

1 head red cabbage, chopped

2 carrots, coarsely grated

$^1/_2$ red onion, sliced into thin crescents

$^1/_2$ cup olive oil

$^1/_2$ cup red wine vinegar

1 clove garlic, crushed

1 tablespoon Dijon mustard

1 teaspoon Oriental sesame oil

salt

pepper

Combine cabbage, carrots, and onion in a bowl. In a separate container, combine remaining ingredients and stir well to mix. Pour marinade over cabbage mixture, stirring well. Cover and refrigerate at least an hour before serving.

Makes 8 servings

59

Summer meals in the Heartland are resplendent with home grown produce: onions, tomatoes, eggplant, a profusion of peppers, lettuce, cabbage, and celery, to name just a few.

Midwesterners are avid gardeners, and in summertime they enjoy eating the fruits (and vegetables) of their labor. Their gardens' output begins in mid-May with rhubarb, which looks like stalks of pink celery, and is followed by a steady succession of berries—strawberries, black and red raspberries, gooseberries, blueberries, cherries, blackberries, and elderberries. At last come the grapes, pears, peaches, and apples.

Fruits are baked into pies, cobblers, and other luscious desserts, used in fruit salads, or else made into jams, jellies, and preserves. Canning is a pragmatic Midwestern tradition, and neat rows of fruit preserves, like colored jewels, line many a pantry shelf in this region. And not just the old standbys like strawberry jam, either—Midwestern cooks are always coming up with new ideas and adaptations of old ones. Consider jalepeño pepper jelly (which has become as popular in the Midwest as it is in the Southwest), rose-hip jam, and cherry or plum preserves, to name just a few.

As for the desserts, strawberry shortcake is an institution in the Heartland that's considered as American as apple pie. Peach pie, cherry turnovers, blueberry cobbler, apple crisp, Brown Betty—these are some of the desserts that grace Heartland tables. Sweet vegetable breads baked with nuts—zucchini bread, pumpkin bread, and carrot cake—are also widely enjoyed (often spread with cream cheese).

All summer, Midwesterners raise a veritable cornucopia of vegetables: lettuce, asparagus, radishes, spinach, onions, peas, cabbage, broccoli, cauliflower, peppers, carrots, Brussels sprouts, tomatoes, potatoes, beets, cucumbers, eggplant, muskmelons, watermelons, string beans, red beans, lima beans, sweet corn, zucchini, acorn squash. They prepare fresh vegetable salads and slaws; steam or sauté vegetable side dishes; bake vegetable casseroles; and make a variety of soups. They also put up tomatoes and corn relish, and pickle cucumbers and watermelon rind. That way, the bounty of summertime can be enjoyed in the dead of winter.

In the summertime, Midwesterners love to grill outside—everything from hamburgers and bratwurst to T-bone and salmon steaks. Barbecued meals are often accompanied by baked potatoes or home fries, hot buttered corn on the cob, pickles, tossed salad with home grown tomatoes, and strawberry shortcake for dessert.

FOODS

*C*orn was unknown in Europe before Christopher Columbus, but Native Americans had already developed hybrids, adapted to different parts of the country, when the first white settlers arrived. Corn grows best in deep rich soil on flat or gently rolling terrain so the roots can grow deep and spread out. It flourishes in hot summers with plenty of sun and rainfall; corn chowder with potatoes (inset) makes a stick-to-the-ribs meal on cold winter days in the Heartland.

The Corn is as High as an Elephant's Eye

The first American settlers learned from the Native Americans how to plant corn, and thus were saved from starvation when their crops of wheat, barley, and peas all failed. Along with beans, dried corn helped feed the pioneers as they pushed their way across the continent, and they planted corn as they settled in the Midwest. Today, the Corn Belt runs smack-dab through the Heartland: 150 million acres of the richest farmland in the world, ranging from eastern Ohio to eastern Kansas, up to Nebraska and South Dakota. This area of less than one percent of the earth's surface produces more than seventy-five percent of the nation's corn, and forty percent of the world's corn.

Even though most of the corn produced in the Midwest is field corn, which is used for animal feeds and cereals, Midwesterners do eat corn in every form imaginable: corn bread, corn chowder, corn fritters, cream of corn soup, scalloped corn salad, corn cakes, corn flakes, corn dogs, corn pudding, corn meal mush, popcorn, caramel corn, grits, corn on the cob, and succotash.

Folk wisdom says to plant corn in the spring "when the oak leaves are as big as squirrel's ears." Then there are the farmers who swear that if you stand in a cornfield on a hot, windless night you can hear the corn grow. And everyone knows that the best time to eat sweet corn is right after it's been picked—ideally, say fresh corn fanatics, you're to run out to the field with a pot of boiling water. Sweet corn is fragile. If not refrigerated, the corn will lose its flavor within twenty-four hours after it's picked, though it will keep for two to three days in a plastic bag in the refrigerator.

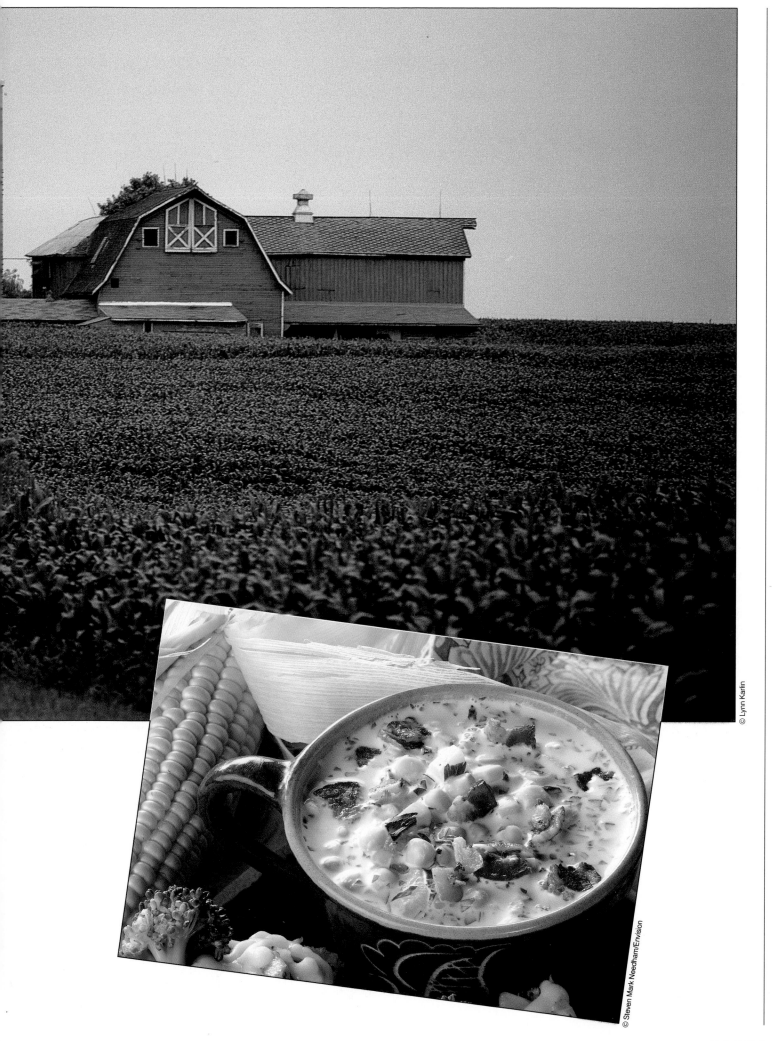

65

© Lynn Karlin

© Steven Mark Needham/Envision

FOODS

THE CORN PALACE

*There is a fabulous Moorish struc-
ture complete with minarets and
kiosks in downtown Mitchell,
South Dakota. Called The Corn
Palace, the building is decorated
inside and out with real corn,
grasses, and grains—3,000 bush-
els, at a cost of $35,000.*

*In June the grasses and grains
are brought in from the fields by
the bushel and nailed onto the sides
of the building. Corn is added in
late August or early September; the
ears are sliced in half and nailed to
the design.*

*Oscar Howe, a Yanktonai
Dakota Sioux, designed The Corn
Palace decorations from 1948 to
1971; he also designed panels for
inside the building. Howe used
Native American motifs and sym-
bolism in his work. Six of his panels were redone for the town's
centennial in 1981, when the
building was dedicated to Howe.*

Fried Green Tomatoes

Frugal Midwestern cooks waste nothing,
so right before the frost hits the pumpkin,
they pick any green tomatoes left in the
garden and fry them up.

6 firm green tomatoes, cut into 1/4-inch slices

1/2 cup buttermilk

1/3 cup flour

1/3 cup cornmeal or 1/3 cup wheatgerm

1/2 teaspoon salt

1/2 teaspoon basil

1/4 teaspoon pepper

1/4 teaspoon thyme

one pinch cayenne (optional)

3 tablespoons olive oil, for frying

1/4 pound Mozzarella cheese, sliced

Mix together flour, cornmeal, and spices.
Dip tomato slices in buttermilk, then
dredge them in the flour mixture. Heat
one tablespoon of oil in a skillet; fry the
tomatoes until golden brown. Add a slice
of Mozzarella cheese and cover the skillet
for the last few minutes of cooking. Add
more oil for the next skillet of tomatoes.
When cooked, tomatoes should be firm
and crisp on the outside, and slightly soft
inside. If the insides fall apart, either the
tomato was getting ripe, or it's been over-
cooked.

Serves 6

Zesty Fresh Tomatoes

Ripe tomatoes

Fresh thyme, to taste

Fresh basil, to taste

Fresh oregano, to taste

Salt to taste

Fresh ground black pepper, to taste

A fast, delicious way to serve tomatoes is
with herbs as a salad, side dish, or snack.
Simply slice ripe tomatoes and place them
flat on a plate. Sprinkle them lightly with
thyme, basil, oregano, salt and pepper.
Use fresh herbs if you have them, but
small pinches of dried herbs are good,
too.

Fresh Boiled Corn

Remember, most people overcook corn
on the cob. Here's how not to. First, boil
sufficient water to cover the corn. Drop
the shucked ears into the water. Let the
water return to a boil. Let the corn cook
no longer than five more minutes.

Roasted Fresh Corn

Plunge unshucked corn into a bucket of
water. Light charcoal in a grill. While the
coals are burning down, pull back the
corn husks almost to the bottom and
remove the silk. Rub each ear with butter
and sprinkle with salt and pepper. Close
the ears back up and tie them with a piece
of string or shuck. When the charcoal is
ready for barbecuing, place the ears on
the grill and cover them with a damp
cloth to keep the steam in. Re-moisten
the cloth as it dries, and keep it far
enough from the coals so it doesn't burn.
Roast the corn for 15 to 20 minutes, turning frequently.

Zucchini Bread

Zucchini is one of the tastiest varieties of summer squash, which is lucky, since it's also one of the most prolific. Midwest gardeners will share a bumper crop of zucchini with friends, neighbors, and coworkers; they have even been known to leave bushel baskets of zucchini by the curb with a sign saying: "Free! Please Help Yourself!" This recipe is an easy way to use up the ubiquitous squash. Serve this quick bread at a party and watch it disappear.

1 cup butter or margarine, softened

2 cups sugar

3 eggs, beaten

2 teaspoons vanilla

2 cups unbleached flour

1/2 cup raw oatmeal

1/2 teaspoon baking powder

2 teaspoons soda

1 teaspoon salt

3 teaspoons cinnamon

1 1/2 teaspoons allspice

*3 cups zucchini, grated
(about 3 medium zucchini)*

1 1/2 cups walnuts, chopped

1 cup raisins

Preheat oven to 350 degrees. Blend butter, sugar, eggs, and vanilla until smooth and creamy. Add remaining ingredients slowly, stirring well to mix. Grease and flour two 8-by-4-inch loaf pans; divide batter evenly between them. Bake for an hour. Allow to cool for at least 10 minutes before removing from pan.

Makes 2 loaves

Sautéed Zucchini in Tomato Sauce

This tangy side dish will complement any meal, year-round. If you don't have the time to make fresh tomato sauce, use packaged tomato or even spaghetti sauce. This recipe makes a good main course when served over pasta.

for the tomato sauce

One 15-ounce-can tomato sauce

1 cup orange juice

2 tablespoons diced onion

4 cloves crushed garlic

1 tablespoon basil

2 teaspoons oregano

1 teaspoon salt

1 teaspoon sugar

1 teaspoon fennel or anise seed

for the zucchini

3 cups zucchini, sliced

3 tablespoons olive oil

1 cup onion, chopped

Combine all ingredients listed under *for the tomato sauce* in a saucepan. Bring to a boil, then reduce heat to low and simmer for at least 1/2 hour.

Using the ingredients under *for the zucchini*, heat olive oil in a heavy skillet and sauté onion until golden. Add sliced zucchini and cover the pan; cook for about 6 minutes, or until tender, shaking the pan regularly to prevent sticking. Remove the lid and add the tomato sauce; cook for 3 minutes.

Serves four

67

HEARTLAND CRAFTS & COLLECTIBLES

The Heartland has a rich heritage of folk art and crafts. The first Midwestern settlers responded with ingenuity and creativity to the challenges of surviving in the wilderness and took pride in creating handsome, sturdily constructed objects to fill their homes. In typical no-nonsense style, contemporary Midwesterners can appreciate artistic ability, but like it to be channeled into creating objects that are practical as well as beautiful.

Accordingly, rustic willow and fine handcrafted wooden furniture, especially Shaker, are popular. Enthusiasm for quilts and other needlework has always been high, because these

72

Folk art based on brush style painting is a tradition all over the Heartland. Styles include Bavarian Bauernmalerei and Scandinavian Rosemaling (above); Quilts and baskets (page 73, top) evoke days gone by; wooden objects (page 73, bottom) are cherished, whether they're carved or painted, flat or three dimensional.

forms allow the crafter to use colored fabric and thread in a way that is comparable to how an artist uses paint. (In recent years this enthusiasm has become almost a mania with some folk art enthusiasts.) Baskets are a perennial favorite, and are used for storing everything from knitting supplies to bath towels. Ceramic tableware, vases, and teapots are common in Midwestern homes, as are handwoven place mats and napkins. Many Heartland residents display collections of antique glassware and pottery, with Rookwood pottery a coveted Midwestern specialty.

Every year at state fairs and craft festivals all over the Midwest you see them: Heartlanders forging and casting metals, making everything from jewelry to weather vanes; carving wooden whirligigs, decoys, pipes, and canes; using tole and decorative painting to embellish furniture, accessories, and walls. You find them practicing fiber arts such as batik, tie dye, and potato print; doing weaving, knitting, needlepoint, and embroidery; crafting pottery and plaiting baskets. Heartlanders in general, and craftspeople in particular, subscribe to this folk wisdom: If it's worth doing, it's worth doing right.

Since pioneer days, Heartlanders have personalized their homes with crafts. Many of these lovingly handmade objects have been passed down through the generations: a quilt made by someone's great-grandmother; a blanket woven of wool from sheep on the family farm; and other family heirlooms, such as needlepoint pillows, embroidered napkins, and tea towels. All these beautiful old objects evoke a sense of the past.

© William Seitz

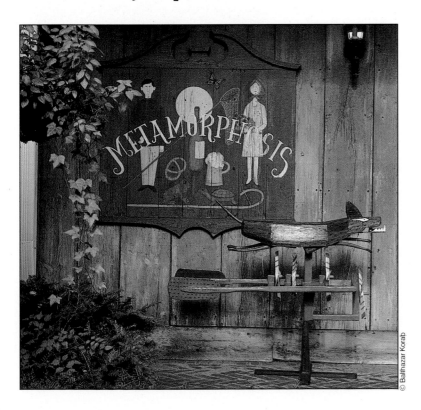

© Balthazar Korab

IN THE WOOD

*T*wig furniture
is quirky and
idiosyncratic, and its
rough, handmade
character is a good
antidote to a hectic
urban life-style. Rustic
pieces are perfectly at
home indoors and out,
and Heartlanders find
ways to incorporate
them in a variety of
decors.

Crafters in the Heartland have been
making rustic twig furniture for hundreds of years, using willow, birch,
cherry, oak, black walnut, or whatever
wood happens to be available. In this
primitive-looking style, twigs, sticks,
branches, logs, and stumps are made
into furniture that's as close as possible
to the wood's original form. Bumps,
twists, and other imperfections are left
in the wood. Crafters rarely work from
a set pattern, but build a piece branch
by branch, taking their cues from the
wood itself. Usually, they'll alternate
from side to side to create a symmetric
design.

   The natural quality of rustic furniture
appeals to Midwestern sensibilities;
style-wise, it works well with the country decors Heartlanders love. Especially
in the southern section of the Heartland that borders Appalachia, crafters
create these one-of-a-kind designs.

   Adirondack-style rustic furniture has
also long been made in the Midwest. It
is more refined looking than rustic
primitive furniture, though it too is
made out of twigs and branches. Deriv-
ing from the carpentry tradition, much
of it was manufactured around the turn
of the century by the Old Hickory
Chair Company in Indiana, which is
now defunct. The company shipped its
rustic-looking hickory wood furniture
with woven rattan seats and chair backs
to many of the great resorts which
flourished in upstate New York, but
much of it stayed in the Heartland, as
well.

CRAFTS AND COLLECTIBLES

Rustic Plant Stand

This twig stand is great for holding house-plants—and it works well on deck, porch, or patio. Make sure to set pots in saucers, however, or you will make a mess when watering plants. (An alternative would be to line the plant stand with a plastic trough, available at garden stores.)

Materials Needed

Four 30-inch-long twigs (1¼-inch diameter)

Four 16-inch-long twigs (1-inch diameter)

Sixteen 20-inch-long twigs (1-inch diameter)

Twenty 12-inch-long twigs (1-inch diameter)

1½-inch flat-head nails

Hammer

Directions

1. Place two 20-inch twigs about eight inches apart, and parallel, on your work surface.

2. Maintaining a one-inch overlap, place a 12-inch twig on each end and nail in place. Repeat this process, alternating between sets of 20-inch and 12-inch twigs, until the planter box reaches the desired height.

3. To add legs, place one of the 30-inch twigs on the inside corner of the planter box and nail in place. Repeat for each corner.

4. To anchor the legs, add a crosspiece 5½ inches off the floor. Nail in place.

5. Secure the back of the planter to the front with two 20-inch twigs.

6. To brace the side of the planter stand, nail on four 16-inch twigs, two on top and two under the horizontal twig.

7. Using two 20-inch twigs, add a V brace to each side. Nail to secure in place.

77

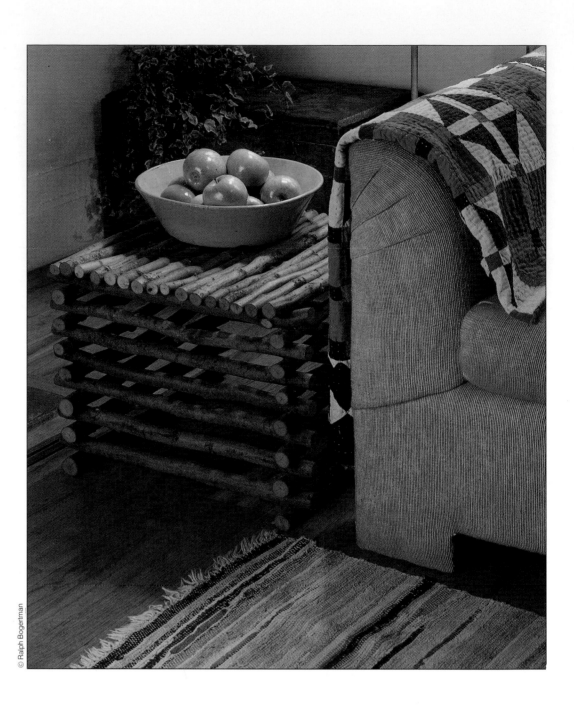

Rustic End Table

This "log-cabin" style table is quick and easy to build, and it adds an authentic country accent to just about any room. (Gathering the sticks is fun, too.)

Materials Needed

Forty-four 20-inch-long twigs, as close to the same diameter as possible. (A $1/2$- to $3/4$-inch diameter works well.)

$1^1/_2$-inch flat-head nails

Hammer

Directions

1. For the bottom, select two twigs of uniform dimension. They should be as flat as possible; sand the bottoms if necessary to ensure stability. Then place two more twigs perpendicularly on top of the first two to make a square, allowing a 1-inch overlap on the sides.

2. Nail the twigs in place. Repeat this process of placing two twigs on top of the preceding twigs, log-cabin style, until you've reached the desired height.

3. Make a top for the table by laying twigs across the top, no more than $1/4$ inch apart. You can use the table as it stands, or cover it with a piece of $1/4$-inch glass with polished edges.

HANDS TO WORK, HEARTS TO GOD

In 1860 the Shaker religion was at its height in the United States. Eighteen settlements, including some in Ohio and Kentucky, boasted six thousand members. Everything the Shakers did or made was intended to glorify God, and everything they created was meant to be used and loved. Their founder, Mother Ann Lee, believed that work should be executed as if you had a thousand years to live, but also as if you were going to die tomorrow.

The Shakers are credited with inventing the flat broom, the automatic spring, the clothes-peg, a metal pen-point, seed packages, the threshing machine, pea-sheller, apple-corer, static electricity machine and the circular saw, among other things. But we remember them most for their beautiful, handcrafted furniture, which stands as a prototype of the "form follows function" dictum, years before that concept was articulated.

The Shakers were among the first to develop the rocking chair, in the 1790s; their Brumby rocker design is still imitated today. As early as 1830, their chairs and rockers were sought after as the best in America. Originals of their simple ladder-back chairs with caned seats now sell for outrageous prices, though handcrafted Shaker-style reproductions or high-quality manufactured reproductions are more affordable.

A STITCH IN TIME

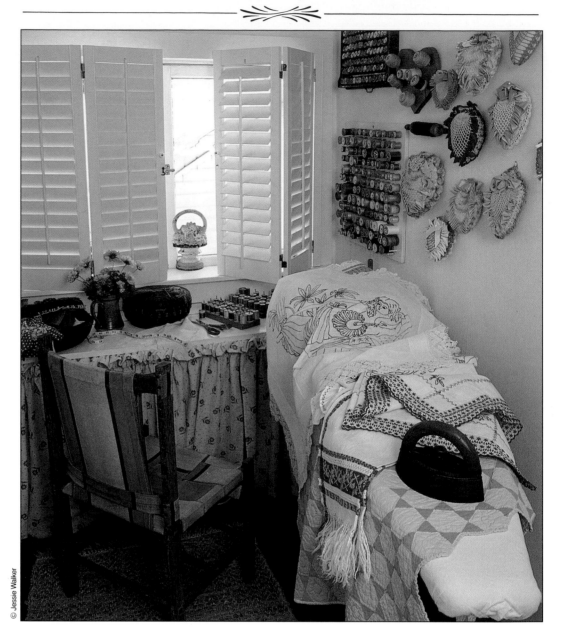

© Jessie Walker

The needle arts—quilting, embroidery, needlepoint, crochet, and knitting—have been a means of personal expression for generations of Heartland women. (Often needlework was the only means of creative expression open to them.) Girls would learn to read and to sew at the same time by cross stitching samplers. Pioneer women frugally saved scraps to make beautiful bedcoverings and quilts that were kaleidoscopes of color and pattern. With needlepoint, women took a mix-and-match approach to color, thread, and stitches. Knitting provided a means of making warm clothing—snuggly sweaters, socks, and hats.

Classic Samplers

Since the sixteenth century in Europe, little girls (and occasionally boys), some as young as four or five, have been sewing samplers, or "examplars." Settlers brought this tradition west on the Conestoga wagons, and used it as an educational tool. Designed to record a repertoire of stitches, samplers usually included an alphabet and some verse, which was often piously moral. Genealogical samplers that have survived are now valuable records, as they list the dates of family members' births, marriages, and deaths, which may not be recorded elsewhere. Whether sewn out of love or out of duty, samplers survive as cultural artifacts of childhood in the past.

Women did—and still do—fine embroidery on tablecloths, napkins, pillowcases, tea towels, pincushions, hot pads, tea cozies, throw pillows, aprons, clothing, and just about anything else you can draw a needle through. Nowadays samplers are sewn mostly by adults, but they use the same French

A Gallery of Needlework Crafts

All of the following forms of needlework have been popular at one time or another in the Midwest; many continue to attract devotees, who sew less out of necessity than because of passionate enthusiasm.

Shelburne Museum, Shelburne, Vermont

This is a prized example of the type of needlework done in nineteenth-century Heartland homes.

knots, bullion knots, outline stitch, running stitch, cross stitch, and chain stitch that little girls and their mothers have been using for centuries. Sometimes, as in the past, embroiderers copy a design from some favorite china or a painting; others buy one of the many kits available or follow a pattern from a book. Favorite subjects continue to be grapes, pomegranates, apples, and cherries; prairie flowers, including red poppies and blue cornflowers; as well as golden wheat, roses, daisies, and irises.

© MacDonald Photography/Envision

Versatile Crewel

This special form of embroidery uses wool yarns on an even-weave fabric to depict scenes from nature—birds, flowers, and landscapes—in a painterly way. Crewel has been used on upholstery, throw pillows, and footstools as well as for wall hangings.

Enduring Knits

Heartlanders have been knitting hats, scarves, sweaters, and socks for their families for generations. Yarn is available in a rainbow of colors and textures, and garments can be knitted in a variety of patterns, so this craft has a versatility and practicality rivaled only by quilts.

Lavish Lace

Tatting and other lacemaking techniques are said to be on the wane, but dedicated Heartlanders are carrying on the traditions—even making bobbin lace and Battenburg lace as their grandmothers and great-grandmothers did. The weaving process is tedious—an inch an hour is good for bobbin lace—and patience is a necessity, not just a virtue, for anyone who wants to make these delicate patterns.

© William Seitz

Crochet Techniques

Afghans are the most frequently crocheted items in the Heartland today, but people are also rediscovering the joy of Victorian lace crochet.

*S*pun from wool,
cotton, linen,
and silk, as well as
synthetics and blends,
yarn is sold in a variety
of weights and colors
(page 82, top). Some
Heartland craftspeople
prefer to spin and dye
their own, even using
natural dyes; crocheted
afghans are an
enduring symbol of love
(page 82, bottom). We
continue to enjoy these
personalized blankets
long after the people
who made them are
gone. Protected from
moths, afghans will last
for generations;
needlepoint (left) lends
itself well to geometric
designs, especially in
upholstery. In general,
pillows and wall
hangings tend to be
more interpretive, with
painterly subjects like
landscapes, still lifes,
and animals.

83

Needlepoint

Needlepoint allows you to use yarn, embroidery floss, pearl cotton, crewel wool, silk, metallic, or linen threads to create a design—and you can mix these various threads, as well. Midwesterners of yesterday and today have created a wide variety of useful, yet beautiful objects for the home using needlepoint techniques. Sewn on special canvas, using separate needles for each color of thread, needlepoint pillows, footstools, rugs, and wall hangings have graced Heartland homes for generations.

Norwegian

This Norwegian counted-thread technique looks like old-fashioned lace, but it's actually embroidery. Used for placemats and napkins, Hardanger is embroidered in blocks of satin stitches, then accented with cutwork and delicate needleweaving.

QUILTS— A LABOR OF LOVE

A mish and Mennonite women make quilts to use, to give as gifts, and to sell. Long prized by collectors, and now recognized as serious folk art, these quilts command high prices (up to $10,000) at auctions throughout the Heartland.

Quilts are classic ingredients of the Midwestern home. They were coveted in the past because they provided not only warmth, but also color and beauty. In addition, quilting bees were both a work and a social occasion, so they provided a chance for lots of women to get together and chat. (In the old days there were also "picking bees" to help clean and untangle the masses of wool in preparation for carding and spinning; "husking bees" to shuck corn for winter storage; as well as apple parings, log rollings, and barn raisings; but quilting bees were special because of the enduringly beautiful quilts they produced.) The "bee" is named after the honey bee, who's so busy all the time.

Quilts consist of three parts: the quilt top, or pattern, made ahead of time and often composed of a series of squares; the lining, or the back, sometimes made of soft flannel; and the interlining, sandwiched between the top and the lining, usually made of cotton batting, or sometimes from an old blanket. These three layers are then bound together by quilting—super-fine stitches in a variety of patterns. This is what the women would sew at the bee: the finished quilt top (or tops—if there was room in the house, a hostess might have her guests work on several at once) was stretched on a quilting frame, which the women clustered around. As they completed the work the quilt was rolled on its frame, forcing the quilters to move closer together, and encouraging them to share secrets. The guests would return until the quilts were completed; thus quilting parties could sometimes last up to ten days.

Many patchwork quilt tops were made from clothes that could no longer be worn; calico was the supreme material. Designs composed of strips or squares were easier to put together, but many women were inventive and creative in their work with these simple shapes, using color to make a statement. Quilt tops might be pieced together in unique designs created by the individual, who would then make a name for her pattern. Or they might

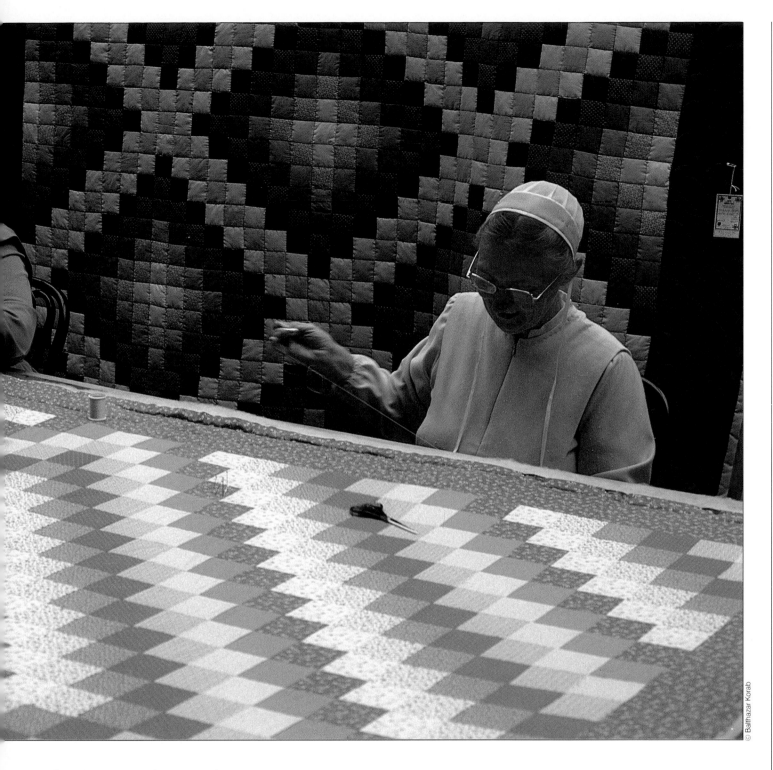

© Balthazar Korab

follow a traditional pattern (the woman could still invent her own name for it). The names of quilts were often inspired by familiar objects and sights—horseshoes, windmills, the classic little red schoolhouse, and the Indian river, for example. And sometimes the quilts' names reflected the hard times pioneers experienced in settling the Heartland. Thus we find quilts with names like Rocky Road to Kansas, Crosses and Losses, Indian Hatchet, and Kansas Dugout.

The star designs were arguably the most popular. Consider the following collection of quilt top designs: the Star of Bethlehem, Star of the East, Eight-Pointed Star, Twinkling Star, Shooting Star, Morning Star, Evening Star, Rising Sun, and Lone Star, even Stars within Stars. Rose names were also popular—Carolina Rose, Rose of Sharon, Prairie Rose, Rose in Bud, and Love Rose, to name a few.

Quilt Top Designs

A standard quilt top design may have several interchangeable names, which can be confusing when it comes to identifying patterns. Name changes were often the result of historical circumstances: Job's Tears became the Slave Chain to reflect the blacks' situation in the South, which eventually became the Endless Chain after the slaves were freed. Multiple names were also due to superstition. For example, Wandering Foot was never included in anyone's dower chest until it was redubbed Turkey Tracks, because the former name was considered bad luck for a bride. These names are whimsical and sometimes even poetic, as the following list illustrates:

Baseballs

Beggars' Blocks

Bear Paw (also known as Duck's Foot in the Mud and Hand of Friendship)

Birds in Flight (also known as Wild Geese Flying)

Block Pattern

Cactus Rose

Cakestand

Chimney Sweep (also known as Courthouse Square)

Crazy Quilt

Crescent Moon

Cupid's Arrowpoints

Dresden Plate

Geometric Snowballs

Grandmother's Flower Garden

Hands over Hearts

Grandmother's Fan

Heart

Hearts and Flowers

Hex Signs

Jacob's Ladder

Job's Tears (also known as Slave Chain and Endless Chain)

I realized that all the really good ideas I'd ever had came to me while I was milking a cow. So I went back to Iowa.
—Grant Wood, painter of American Gothic

Linked Wedding Rings

Log Cabin

Lovers' Knots

Lotus Flower

Oak Leaf

Postage Stamp

Pyramid

Robbing Peter to Pay Paul

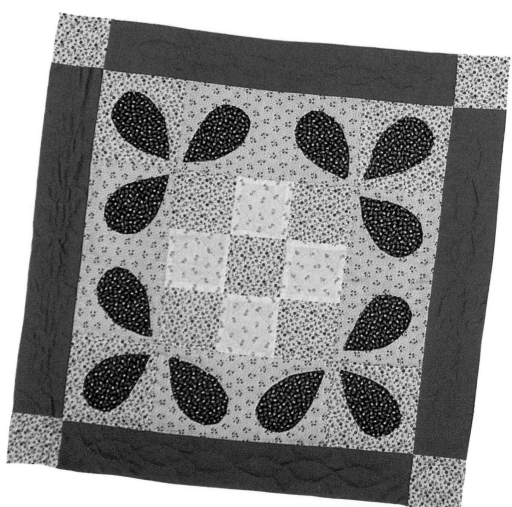

87

Rose of Sharon

Star of Bethlehem

Square-in-Square

Sunburst

Tumbling Blocks

Wandering Foot (also known as Turkey
Tracks and Death's Black Darts)

Wild Goose Chase

Quilting Stitches

The quilting stitch had to be compatible with the quilt top designs, and this was where good seamstresses were really in demand. Women would compete to see who could make the tiniest stitches. Elaborate designs, like those in the following list, were drawn with the help of templates; an especially intricate design might use up to twelve thousand yards of thread. Simpler designs, such as the diagonal, crossbar, double crossbar, and the diamond, could be stitched freehand. Sometimes quilters would simply outline the pattern of the quilt top, stitching $1/8$- to $1/4$-inch on either side of a seamline.

Acanthus

Daisy

Day Lily

Heart

Feather

Fan

Oak Leaf

Peacock Fan

Pineapple

Princess Feather

Running Vine

Shell

Spiderweb

Star and Crown

Starfish

Swirl

Teacup

88

The quilt [top] might have been made years before and folded away in the dower chest. But invitations to a quilting where the heart design was employed was tantamount to an engagement announcement. For hearts were the insignia of a bride and up until 1940 such a design used in any quilt other than that of a bride was considered unlucky and presaged that dire disaster of a broken engagement.
—*Thomas Hamilton Ormsbee,* Collecting Antiques in America

Pattern For Ohio Star Quilt

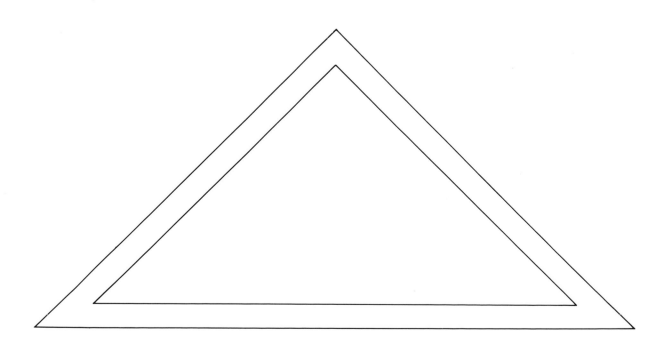

OHIO STAR WALL HANGING

Making this 15-inch-by-15-inch quilt block wall hanging will acquaint you with the basics of quilting. If you find yourself hungry for more, once you have completed this project, consider making a quilt coverlet by repeating the block side by side (*see diagrams 10, 11*). Or you might subdivide the block and create a whole new look (*see diagram 12*). The possibilities and color choices are endless, challenging, and lots of fun.

Materials Needed

²/₃-yard "white" fabric*

¹/₄-yard "blue" fabric*, or scraps

¹/₄-yard "yellow" fabric*, or scraps

Iron and ironing board

Pencils

Tracing paper

Poster board

Glue

Scissors

Sewing machine

Neutral color, all-purpose thread

20-inch square of quilt batting

Hand quilting needles (betweens)

Quilting thread

Straight pins

2 plastic cafe curtain rings

¹/₄-inch masking tape, optional

Quilting hoop, optional

*These fabric colors are listed for convenience of description only. Please choose colors that please you, and match your decor (*see diagrams 8, 9*).

Prewash fabrics in cold water to avoid later shrinkage and to test for color fastness. Press fabric. (Note: Wash finished wall hanging in *cold water only*. Warm water can cause the fabric to bleed.)

1. The Ohio Star quilt block is made up of 16 triangles and 5 squares (see diagram 1). The pattern pieces, or templates, for these shapes are drawn up here in actual size. Trace them exactly, using a sharp pencil.

2. Glue the tracing paper onto the posterboard; cut through both layers along the outline of the template. It's very important to make accurate templates or the quilt block may not fit together or lay flat at the end.

3. From the "white" fabric cut a 20-inch square to use later as the back of the quilt block.

4. Using a sharp pencil to outline the triangle template, mark and then cut 4 "white" triangles, 4 "yellow" triangles, and 8 "blue" triangles.

5. Using the square template, mark and then cut 4 "white" squares and 1 "blue" square. Make sure you line up the templates along the straight grain of the fabric. (Since these templates have the seam allowance already built into them, it is permissible to mark on either the right or the wrong side of the fabric, as long as you are consistent throughout. The marking lines disappear when you cut through them with the scissors.)

continued on next page

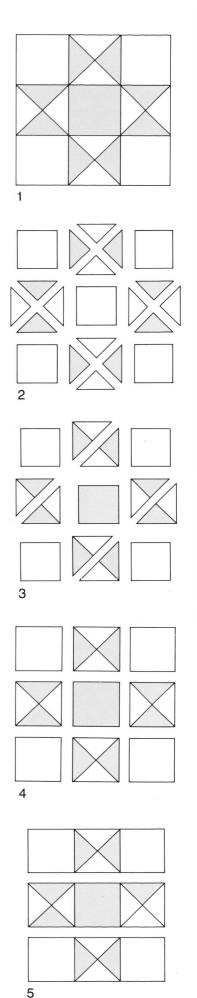

1

2

3

4

5

91

*C*olorful quilts on the walls not only look great, but act as soundproofing and insulation, too. When they aren't on display, quilts should be carefully stored. To store an old quilt, roll it on a large cardboard tube, cover it with a bedsheet, and store it in a dry, well-ventilated area.

94

© Jessie Walker

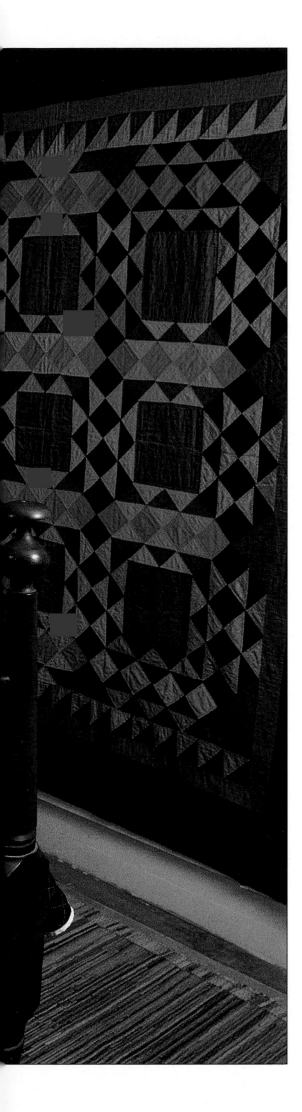

QUILT LORE

In the past, it was the custom for a girl to complete twelve or thirteen quilt tops for her dower chest. When she became engaged her mother would hold a quilting bee and the quilts would be completed. Sometimes the twelfth quilt was supplied by the groom, made by his sister or mother, and was called a Freedom quilt. It was usually made in red, white, and blue, with a pattern that featured eagles, stars and stripes, or some other patriotic symbol. The thirteenth quilt, or bride's quilt, was usually made for the girl by her mother, aunt, or other relative, and was often the finest of all. Traditional patterns included the Wedding Ring (for virginity), and Oak Leaves (for longevity).

Other quilts, called presentation quilts, were collaborative efforts made for a prominent person, such as a teacher or a minister. Often, each square was made by a different person, friend or relative, and carried an appropriate message, usually signed.

Another interesting quilt was the legacy quilt, made up of squares with all the different designs a woman loved. The woman might then decide to do an entire quilt in one of the patterns she particularly enjoyed piecing.

Among the most remarkable quilts are those made by the "plain people." These Amish and Mennonite quilts are famous for their fine craftsmanship, jewellike colors—they use only solid colors, no prints— and their special attention to pattern. Designs and techniques are still passed from generation to generation, and since women from these communities are only allowed to sew functional items, all their creativity is channeled into this form. Their unique quilts are coveted by both dealers and collectors.

95

Step 2

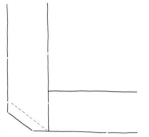

Step 3

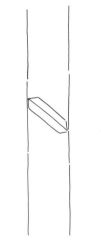

Step 3

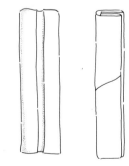

Step 4

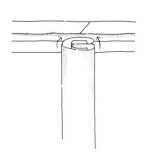

Step 5

THE CHARM OF HANDMADE RUGS

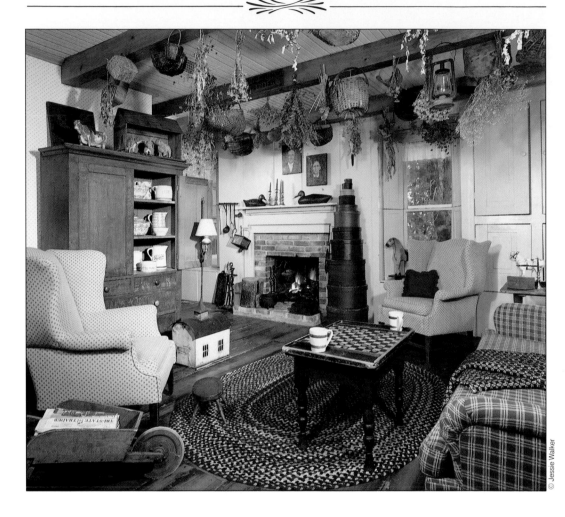

Heartlanders know that handmade rugs help create a cozy atmosphere, a downhome feeling of old-fashioned hospitality. These rugs can be hooked, braided, needlepointed, or appliqued. Whether they're in front of the fire, covering a hardwood floor, or inside the front door, these rugs provide welcome warmth. Midwesterners have been making rugs since pioneer days, and they aren't about to stop now. A colorful prairie rug made of felt and appliqued with designs of birds, flowers, hearts, and other patterns can become the focal point of a room; a braided rug, as described in the following project, might simply provide a country accent.

BRAIDED RAG RUG

The same philosophy of "waste not, want not" that produced the crazy quilt inspired rag rugs. They were created by thrifty Midwestern forebearers as a way to utilize old fabric that was too worn or unattractive to be used in a quilt. This project will produce a small (22-inch diameter) round rug; for a larger one, simply collect more rags. In selecting your fabrics, choose colors that look especially good grouped closely together. Try to find material that is about the same weight.

Materials Needed

5 pounds of rags, heavy to medium weight fabric (wool or cotton are most authentic)

Tailor's chalk

Yard stick

Sharp scissors

Iron

Sewing machine (can sew by hand, if necessary)

Needle

Linen thread

Directions

1. *Mark 2¹/₂-inch wide strips of fabric with tailor's chalk, using the yard stick as a guide. Cut strips along the grain.*

2. *Machine stitch strips together on the bias by placing the end of one strip on top of and perpendicular to the other.*

3. *Trim seams to ¹/₄-inch; press open.*

4. *Fold the outer edges of each strip toward the center, so the edges meet. Then fold the strip again so the folded edges meet, creating four thicknesses of fabric. Steam press to set the folds; roll each folded strip around itself to form a wheel.*

5. *Sew two separate strips together as you did above: Place one strip on top of and perpendicular to the other, then stitch on the bias. Lay the joined strips flat; place the end of a third strip between the fold of the first two to make a T-shape. As you braid, always keep the open edges of each strip to the left.*

6. *Begin braiding by lifting the right strand over the center strand. Then lift the left strand over the new center strand. Continue like this, keeping an even tension, but without stretching the braid. Stitch new strips to the working strips as necessary and continue braiding.*

7. *Sew the braids together using heavy thread and a strong needle. Beginning at the center, insert the needle into a space on the rug with an upward stroke, then pick up the loop on the braid with a downward stroke. Sewing it this way interlocks the braid instead of just stitching it side by side. Your next upstroke picks up the adjacent strand of the adjacent braid. Stitch every loop except on curves, where you should skip every other loop.*

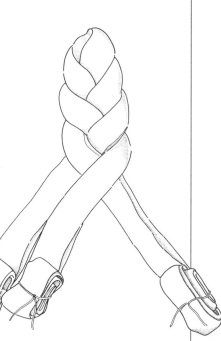

Step 6 Broken Down

97

ORGANIC DYES

Weavers sometimes card and spin their own wool; for colors other than those provided by the sheep, they'll use dyes, often from natural sources. A wealth of practical knowledge comes down to us from the experiments of Heartland pioneers, who skillfully used natural dyes to color their fabrics.

The most common natural dye hues are browns, yellows, greens, oranges, and violets. Reds and blues are hard to come by, but Heartlanders continue to experiment. (A friend once used mulberries to create a lovely deep magenta.) Hollyhocks and madderroot produce lush reds, and dandelion roots yield magenta; pokeberries impart a lavender shade, while sumac yields gray. Cocklebur gives a deep gold; marigolds make orange; and hickory bark, yellow. Midwestern crafters continue to try different flowers, leaves, grasses, seeds, barks, roots, hulls, pods, stems, twigs, and vines to see what colors they can make.

Sometimes the same dye stuff yields several colors, depending on the mordant—the chemical that acts as a fixative to keep the color stable. Onion skins, for instance, produce yellow, brown, rust, and green.

WEAVERS' WEBS

Yet another craft drawn from the pioneer tradition is weaving, both on-loom and off. On-loom weaving requires a space large enough to hold the loom (which is generally quite large), a meticulously planned design and quite a bit of setup and work time. Originally used to make fabric for clothing, shawls, rugs, and bedcoverings, the weaving technique is also employed by modern Heartland weavers to make tablecloths, place mats, napkins, wallhangings, and tapestries.

Off-loom weaving can be more impromptu. Although it's difficult to weave fabric wide enough to use in constructing clothing, you can make a variety of small panels, runners, rugs, and hangings without a loom. And basketmaking is actually a form of off-loom weaving. Weavers use a variety of plant fibers—including willow, cane, hemp, honeysuckle, grape vines, and grasses—to twine, coil, and plait baskets of various sizes and shapes. Drawing on Shaker, Indian, and other basketry traditions, Heartland crafters produce a variety of beautiful woven containers, ranging from practical objects to pure art. (Galleries in cities like Chicago and St. Louis sell one-of-a-kind Heartland baskets for thousands of dollars.)

© E.A. McGee/FPG International

*W*eaving, the ancient process of forming cloth on a loom by interweaving threads, is alive and well in the Heartland. A loom works by holding warp threads taut, then alternately raising and lowering them to create a shed for the weft (or woof) threads to pass through.

99

CRASTS FROM THE GARDEN

Because their gardens are so important to them, Midwesterners are fond of crafting home decorations made from plants. Wreaths of dried flowers, herbs, and vines as well as dried flower bouquets grace doors, windows, and tabletops in their homes. Heartlanders in the western Breadbasket use wheat to make a variety of decorations, including delightful prairie Christmas trees, harvest dolls, and wall hangings.

Pressed flowers are used in a variety of craft projects: framed collages, greeting cards, sun catchers (flowers pressed between glass and hung in a window),

and serving trays or coasters. Yellow and pink flowers usually retain color well, while red ones tend to turn brown, and blue flowers often turn pale pink or beige. Pansy, black-eyed susan, cosmos, daisy, heather, lavender, Queen Anne's lace, tansy, and zinnia all press well. To press flowers, place them between sheets of white blotting paper, and sandwich the blotter between sheets of corrugated cardboard. Place on a flat surface, then stack heavy books on top and leave for at least two weeks. Tweezers are useful for handling the pressed flowers them in craft projects.

*D*ried flowers add color, texture, and vitality to an interior. To keep them from shedding, mist them lightly with hair spray or artist's fixative; for lasting color, keep them out of bright sunlight. Preserve flowers by hanging them upside down in a cool, dry, dark place. Darkness isn't mandatory, but colors fade faster in light. Dried flowers can be used in potpourris, arrangements, and wreaths—some Heartland weddings even use dried flowers instead of fresh flowers.

© Balthazar Korab

HOW TO DRY FRESH FLOWERS

To dry fresh herbs and flowers, pick them before they are fully mature. The simplest drying technique is to hang them upside down in a dry, well-ventilated room. Or you can place about an inch of silica gel in a pan, place the flowers on top, then carefully cover the flowers with more silica gel. Put the box in a warm place for several weeks until all the moisture is removed. The silica gel prevents the flowers' petals

from withering, and helps retain the blossoms' original shape. The drying process can be speeded up somewhat by placing the pan with flowers and silica gel in a 200 degree oven for several hours. Continually check the flowers to see if moisture has evaporated. Some people even use the microwave, which cuts the drying time to two minutes. When using the microwave, however, you must also put a coffee cup full of water in the oven; the moisture will keep the flowers from burning.

CRAFTS AND COLLECTIBLES

That irregular and intimate quality of things made entirely by the human hand.
—Willa Cather,
Death Comes for the Archbishop

Directions

1. Make a hanger for the wreath by twisting florist wire around the straw base, creating a loop. Then wire small clusters of flowers or herbs onto florist's picks and push them into the inner and outer edges of the wreath. Fill in the spaces between these clusters with small bunches of another flower or herb. Continue filling in the wreath with dried plants (some may be easier to secure with U-shaped pins), distributing colors and textures in a pleasing arrangement. Fill in any gaps with single flowers. Add a bow, if you like.

2. A variation of this wreath of mixed herbs and flowers is to select one flower as your background. (In recipe III. above, for instance, artemisia would make a good choice.) If you choose to do this, remember to assemble more of the background material and fewer of the other flowers. Attach your background material first, clustering several short springs and attaching them with U-shaped pins or florist picks. Work in the same direction all the way around so that everything points the same way. Scatter your accent flowers evenly throughout the wreath, securing with florist picks or U-shaped pins.

DRIED HERBAL WREATH

An herbal wreath can be made from a wide variety of herbs and dried flowers. Use or adapt one of the suggested combinations below, or make up your own, using whatever herbs and flowers are available in your own garden.

I.

Baby's breath

Blue statice

Golden yarrow

Hydrangea

Lavender

Mint

Pink rosebuds

Rose yarrow

Santolina

Tansy

White statice

Yellow rosebuds

II.

Cinnamon stick

Golden rod

Pinecones

Rabbit tobacco

Rosemary

Siberian seedpods

Yarrow

III.

Artemisia

Astilbe

Baby's breath

Lunaria

Oregano flowers

Strawflowers

Tansy

Teasel

Yarrow

IV.

Anise

Basil

Dill

Garlic (whole cloves)

Marjoram

Oregano

Parsley

Red peppers

Tarragon

Thyme

Sage

Materials Needed

Straw wreath base

Florist wire

Florist picks

U-shaped pins

Bow (optional)

*Whatever is fashioned, [let] it be plain and simple… unembellished by any superfluities which add nothing to its goodness or durability.
—Mother Ann Lee, founder of the Shakers*

103

CRAFTS AND COLLECTIBLES

FOLK ART

Folk art is egalitarian: art by and for the common people. Although it's often crude and childlike, even primitive looking, folk art represents a spontaneous aesthetic desire, an assertion of individuality. Unconcerned with the laws of perspective or specific artistic doctrines, folk artists make their own rules.

Generally used to describe paintings and wood carvings, the term folk art can also be interpreted more broadly, to include handmade objects designed for use—thus, much of what we've covered so far in this chapter qualifies. Weather vanes, decoys, whirligigs, dolls, and handpainted furniture are just a few more possibilities. Although folk art objects are crafted in every region of the United States, Midwestern designs are distinguished by their Heartland motifs.

Weather vanes were manufactured, but Heartland farmers would often make their own by cutting the outline of a favorite animal from a sheet of metal. Thus you'll find weather vanes in the shapes of cows, sheep, horses, and roosters, as well as more fanciful ones shaped like Indians, butterflies, and reindeer.

Decoys are another important folk art. The Native Americans were probably the first to use bird lures in a systematic way, but this style of hunting was also adopted by the white settlers. Unlike the Native Americans, however, who made birds of grass and attached the dried heads of real waterfowl, the settlers carved and painted decoys which were hollowed out and then weighted. Hunters all over the Heartland practiced this craft, but especially in the Great Lakes region. Nowadays, though folk artists still make authentic decoys, they are used largely for decoration.

107

Folk art whirligigs (often called windmills in the Heartland) have been carved since the early 1800s. Originally used to scare birds away from the garden, whirligigs are often made in the shapes of people or animals, with propellers that catch the breeze and make the figures move.

Dolls are a form of folk art unto themselves. Little girls whose families couldn't afford fancy store-bought china dolls would have homemade specimens instead: carved wooden dolls, rag dolls, dried apple-head dolls, and corn husk dolls.

This detail of handpainted wood shows how decorative painting interprets the forms of nature in a stylized way. The characteristic brush work expresses vitality and a sense of movement.

*C*arving decoys (right) is one of the Heartland's oldest folk art traditions. It evolved from Native American hunting practices, and has become a decorative art unto itself; the Heartland has recently experienced a resurgence of interest in the art of decorative painting. Anything and everything can be painted: bowls, trays, utensils, furniture, accessories, walls, doors, and fabrics.

108

© Paul T. McMahon/Heartland Images

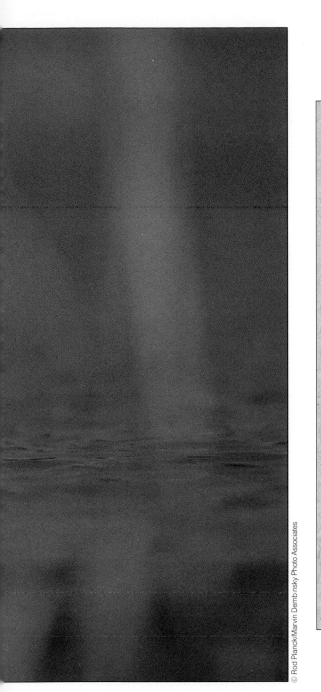

DECORATIVE FOLK PAINTING

Various styles of decorative painting were applied to household goods in Europe for centuries, and Old World folk artists brought their decorative traditions with them when they immigrated to America and settled in the Heartland. These folk painters embellished tables, chairs, stools, chests, beds, dressers, boxes, trays—even walls and occasionally fabrics—with flowers, birds, animals, and symbols. Sometimes using stencils but most often painting freehand, decorative artists worked on tin, wood, and ceramic surfaces to raise everyday objects to the level of art. Rosemaling decorative painting came from rural Scandinavia and featured colorful floral designs and inscriptions painted on furniture, walls, and wooden dinnerware. Traditional design colors include medium greens, reds, white, yellow, and blue, often outlined in yellow ochre; typical background colors include grayish blues, blue greens, dull reds, and red orange. However, modern practitioners of this folk art are not necessarily restrained by tradition. Rosemalers today may use any colors that suit their fancy, or shades that work well in a particular design.

German fraktur, *or "fractured" style writing, is descended from medieval calligraphy. In addition to letters, this unique form of illuminated writing features a special iconography of birds, flowers, and geometric symbols.* Fraktur *found its way to the Heartland with immigrating Germans, some of whom moved first to Pennsylvania Dutch country. Used to decorate birth, baptismal, and marriage certificates as well as pottery, tinware, and furniture, this style of painting featured bright reds, yellows, and greens; a favorite motif combined a rose and a tulip.*

HEARTLAND GARDENS

Heartlanders are avid gardeners. Even though more of them now reside in cities than in the country, many Heartlanders have their roots on the farm. Gardening is a way of staying in touch with the cycle of the seasons, enacting the ancient ritual of sowing seeds, tending the plants, and finally, harvesting the crop.

Given the region's rich soil and lengthy growing season, just about any plant will flourish, so growing a variety of plants is relatively easy. Predictably, pragmatic Midwesterners have always favored large vegetable gardens over any other kind. But even vegetables go in and out of fashion: Onions and lettuce have

© Derek Fell

In early spring, gardeners put in the first hardy root crops, leafy greens, and cabbage. Then come the tender crops— tomatoes, peppers, okra, and squash. Freshly harvested produce must be tasted to be believed (above). Tulips (opposite) come in a rainbow of colors and a variety of shapes as well. The world's biggest tulip farm is in Holland, Michigan— seventy-five acres owned by the Veldheer family.

been steadily gaining ground over the past few years, and corn is losing its popularity.

Every summer, Midwestern gardeners are rewarded with a cornucopia of produce: carrots, radishes, peppers, beets, cabbage, broccoli, tomatoes, Brussels sprouts, cucumbers, watermelons, and string, lima, and red beans—the staples of the American dinner table.

Heartlanders decorate their springtime gardens with a lovely mix of annuals: Marigolds, snapdragons, geraniums, zinnias, pansies, and petunias are among the most popular.

As the year progresses and some annuals start to droop, Heartlanders turn to chrysanthemums to brighten their gardens. Mums are available in a dazzling array of colors, shapes, and sizes: petite yellow pom poms, giant coral and peach blooms, and spiky white blossoms.

Fall is also the time for planting spring bulbs —typically crocuses, tulips, hyacinths, and daffodils. Other spring bulbs include the eranthis, which resembles a buttercup, or winter aconite, which can push through the snow along with the blue, star-shaped chionodoxa (glory of the snow), and galanthus (snowdrops). Summer blooming bulbs to be planted in the fall include lilies, anemones, alliums, and Dutch iris. Instead of planting rows of bulbs, Heartlanders often opt for clusters of flowers, planting from five to fifteen bulbs in each spot.

Midwestern gardeners are also experimenting with a number of planting and maintenance techniques. Organic gardening uses no artificial pesticides, herbicides, or fertilizers—factors that appeal to the Midwestern no-nonsense sensibility. In raised bed gardens, plenty of organic matter (such as cow manure, compost, or peat) is mixed with the soil, which is then piled up to about a foot high in various beds, with walkways in between. The beds are usually enclosed with railroad ties or boards, and are never walked on, so the soil is never compacted.

Wide row gardening consists of rows about three feet wide with paths on either side. Unlike raised beds, wide row gardens require no boards or lumber to hold the beds in place. By planting vegetables and flowers alternately, wide row gardeners often manage to confuse insects, who then go elsewhere for meals. When low crops are planted to form a cover, wide row gardens require very little maintenance.

© Balthazar Korab

113

RIVERSIDE: THE GARDEN SUBURB

With the opening of the Erie Canal in 1825 and the arrival of the railroads in 1852, Chicago became rapidly industrialized and overcrowded. It was then that the idea of the suburb was born. A fresh concept at the time, the suburb was connected to the city by trolley car or train. It offered easy access to the city as well as the rustic pleasures of the countryside.

In 1868–1870, the landscape architects Frederick Law Olmsted and Calvert Vaux designed the suburb of Riverside just outside of Chicago. One of the first model communities in America and perhaps the most famous, Riverside is the quintessential romantic suburb. Olmsted and Vaux were leaders in the then new profession of landscape architecture. In designing Riverside, they broke with the tradition of the American grid system and instead opted for winding, tree-lined streets and single-family homes surrounded by lawns. They emphasized natural features—such as preserving the riverfront as a public space—and created a parklike setting in which all of the community is part of a great garden.

© Robert Lima/Envision

*A swarm of bees
in May
Is worth a load
of hay;
A swarm of bees
in June
Is worth a
silver spoon;
A swarm of bees
in July
Is not worth a fly.*
—Anonymous

*S*pringtime
perennial gardens
*delight the eyes with
color, and sweet flower
essences waft on cool
breezes.*

THE HEARTLAND HERB GARDEN

Even if it's just a patch of mint or a planter of basil, today's Heartlanders are growing more herbs than ever. Beautiful, fragrant, and useful, too, herbs fit well with pragmatic Midwestern priorities. Herbs are often used to enliven the flavors of other home-grown produce.

Culinary herb gardens typically feature basil, chives, dill, fennel, marjoram, parsley, thyme, and tarragon; you also might find angelica, chervil, oregano, rosemary, and sage. Many of these herbs were grown and treasured by Midwestern pioneers. Medicinal and scented herb gardens also have long and venerable histories. A medicinal garden might include sorrel, parsley, lemon verbena, periwinkle, mallow, borage, thyme, and mint; a scented garden, rose, lavender, lemon thyme, bee balm, and woodruff. Many herbs—such as madder and elderberry—yield colors for dyes, and these were staples in the pioneer plot.

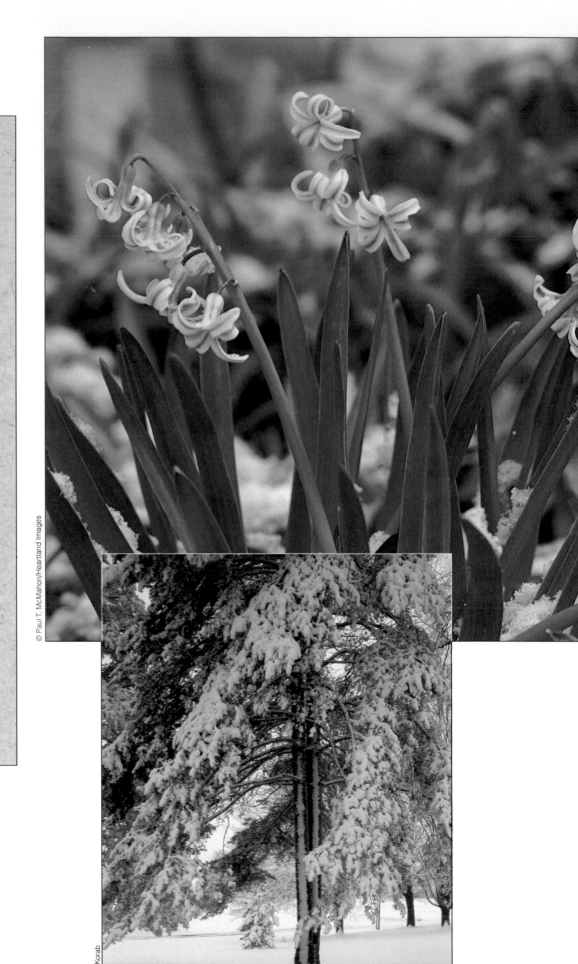

© Paul T. McMahon/Heartland Images

© Balthazar Korab

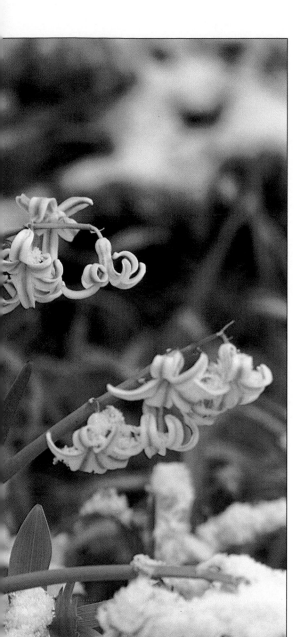

HOW DOES YOUR GARDEN GROW?

The Heartland covers such a vast territory that it actually encompasses several distinct climatic regions. According to *The Old Farmer's Almanac*, these regions are the central Great Plains, the northern Great Plains-Great Lakes, Chicago and southern Great Lakes, and the Greater Ohio Valley.

The eastern-most section, the Greater Ohio Valley, is really deciduous woodland, though many of the trees have been cut down. (Legend has it that in the time before the white man came and cleared the land, a squirrel could hop from the eastern side of the state of Ohio to the western side without touching the ground.) The soil in the eastern Heartland is slightly acid, but the growing season is longer than elsewhere in the Midwest.

In the eastern prairie (the eastern sections of Kansas, Nebraska, and the Dakotas) the soil is rich and loamy. It retains moisture, producing excellent growth with less than optimum precipitation. The weather is extreme—harsh cold, intense heat, and violent storms—but winters are dry, eliminating the main causes of winterkill, while less summer humidity helps control fungus growth.

In the northern portions of Michigan, Minnesota, and Wisconsin the growing season is short and cool. Come winter, the northern Heartland experiences some of the coldest temperatures of this continent, so hardiness becomes the deciding factor in choosing perennials. In the southern parts of these states and Illinois, or what *The Farmer's Almanac* refers to as "Southern Great Lakes," the weather is slightly less severe.

Heartlanders know that an early thaw doesn't always last. Still, it's shocking and sad to see the first spring flowers covered with snow (top). Next year these flowers will bloom again; after a snowfall there is a hush. The world is transformed into a fairy tale. Snow muffles sound, but heightens the other senses.

117

The taste of fresh homegrown tomatoes can't be compared to that of the hard, dry tomatoes sold in supermarkets. Not to mention that tomatoes from the garden come in many more shapes and sizes than are available commercially.

With such variety, about all one can say for sure is that different varieties and hybrids will flourish in different parts of the Heartland. Surveys show that Midwesterners grow more vegetables than anything else, and that tomatoes are the most popular crop of backyard gardeners. The best way to find out which strains grow well in your area is to talk to other local gardeners, or call your local agricultural extension agent.

That's what contributing editor Jan Riggenbach did in her "Your Garden" column for *Midwest Living* magazine in the February 1990 issue. She asked university extension-service and agricultural specialists in each Heartland state to nominate champion varieties for vegetable gardens. The first choice tomatoes were 'Jet Star,' cited for their size, flavor, and crack-resistance by experts in four different states (Iowa, Kansas, Ohio, Wisconsin); other favorites included Supersonic tomatoes (Illinois), 'Show-me' (where else but Missouri), 'Heartland' (Nebraska), 'Celebrity' (second choice of Wisconsin and Iowa), 'Quick Pick' and 'Floramerica' (North Dakota), and 'Rushmore'—which ripen in just sixty to sixty-five days (South Dakota).

In addition, 'Country Fair 87' cucumbers were highly praised by agents in Iowa and Nebraska. 'Silver Queen' sweet corn is popular in the southern part of the Heartland.

© Derek Fell

L *ilies (top) add sparkle to partially shaded areas, and are great for informal arrangements. Every year these perennials come back in bigger clumps, and with more flowers; roses (bottom) have inspired poets, lovers, and gardeners for centuries. They have been written and sung about, strewn along the path, and cried over; they come in a mind-boggling array of hybrid varieties.*

Perennial Favorites

Roses have been the most prized flower in the Heartland for decades, nurtured with an enthusiasm that sometimes borders on mania. But although roses are still the number one flower, they may be on the way out. Black spot disease problems and high maintenance (frequent pruning and fertilization) are driving gardeners away from the queen of flowers; many Midwesterners are cultivating a variety of perennials instead.

Perennials come back every year and can be used in many ways in the yard. For instance, more and more hostas are being planted in the shady spots under trees, while irises and day lilies put on big shows with very little effort on the gardener's part. Also, as Midwesterners slowly move away from grass lawns, perennials are a natural choice for ground covers.

Perennial gardens should be skillfully designed taking into account height, colors, and blooming times. Then the gardener must be patient, waiting at least a year for flowers to bloom.

As you might guess, not all perennials are suited to every corner of the Heartland. But a good way to learn what flowers will grow in your area is to look around. Look at what your neighbors are growing, and as Patricia Thorpe suggests in her book *The American Weekend Garden*, if you can find old gardens, abandoned or neglected, and see what plants thrive, you'll have a good idea as to what plants will flourish.

© Wanda LaRock/Envision

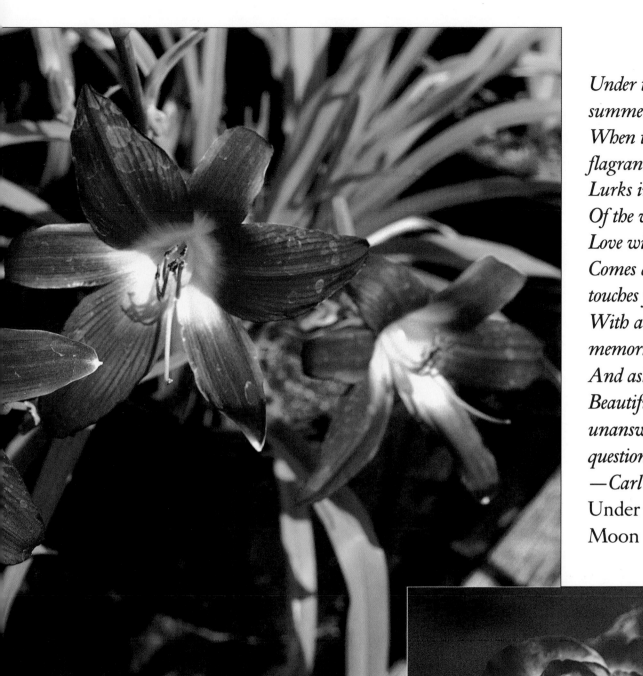

*Under the
summer roses
When the
flagrant crimson
Lurks in the dusk
Of the wild red leaves
Love with little hands,
Comes and
touches you
With a thousand
memories
And asks you
Beautiful
unanswerable
questions.
—Carl Sandburg,*
Under the Harvest
Moon

© D. Long/Envision

*I*t's a sure sign of summer when Queen Anne's lace (above) blooms in wild meadows across the Heartland. Folklore has it that Queen Anne pricked her finger while making lace, and a drop of blood fell. That's why there is a deep red or purple spot in the middle of the flower. Blooming dandelions and violets (page 123) are harbingers of spring in the Midwest.

For many years the well-kept lawn has been a symbol of the American Dream. But this is changing, as Heartlanders tire of endless maintenance and seek attractive alternatives to the swath of green.

Wildflower meadows are a popular option. They have a timeless appeal, and are especially appropriate in the Midwest, as they re-create the look of the wild prairie. Once established, they need very little maintenance. Just mow them once a year. The trick is to buy a blend of seeds created especially for the Heartland, and to thoroughly prepare the soil. A good mix includes annuals as well as perennials, because the latter may take up to three years to bloom. Annuals produce flowers the first year

and often will reseed themselves. (See "A Rainbow of Native Wildflowers," page 126, for the best species to plant.)

Any dedicated gardener knows you must take preliminary steps before planting anything. For a meadow, you must choose a site that receives sunlight for at least three-quarters of the daylight hours. Have the soil tested by an agronomist, or send a sample to the local cooperative extension service. You will be advised as to what soil amendments, if any, are needed to sustain a meadow garden. Then the ground should be worked as if you were planting a lawn, turning the earth over and breaking up the clumps. Broadcast the seed using a lawn seed spreader or by casting the seed evenly over the open ground. A trick to help with this "even spreading" is to mix the seed with sand or garden loam in a proportion of one packet of seeds to four cups sand. Put this mixture in a container with a pour spout (such as a half-gallon milk carton), and shake it vigorously to disperse the seed. Then broadcast the seed from the container. This technique works well with any small seeds, such as spinach or carrot.

Wildflowers make magnificent—if short-lived—fresh bouquets. A more reliable way to preserve their beauty is to dry them for arrangements or wreaths (see page 102). Once established, a wildflower planting only needs to be mowed once a year—in spring or autumn—to keep trees and woody plants from gaining a toehold.

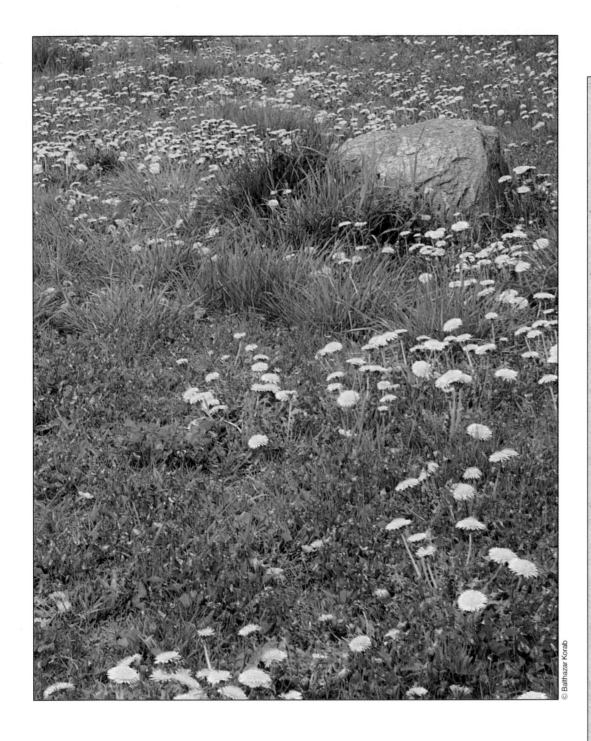

THE MIDWESTERN PRAIRIE

When French explorers in North America first confronted the vast, almost treeless tracts of grassland in the middle of the country, they gave them the all-encompassing name prairie, meaning meadow, from the French praerie.

Prairies are actually intricate ecosystems that support a complex array of plant and animal life. On the prairie grow native grasses and forbs, which are flowering herbaceous plants, as well as shrubs and occasional groups of trees.

There are three major prairie divisions within the United States, each characterized by its own plant species. The shortgrass prairie is located on high plains in the Rocky Mountains. Because rainfall here is limited, the plants that grow there are stunted in size. Farther eastward is the mid-grass prairie, where rainfall is greater and, accordingly, plants grow taller— but this area does not fall significantly within midwestern states.

The tall-grass prairie, sometimes referred to as the "true prairie," is the heart of the Midwest. It runs through every midwestern state and is the most meadowlike and lush of all the prairies. Here plants flourish and may grow several feet high. Within the tall-grass prairie, soil conditions vary greatly—from dry, sandy soil to organically rich soil with good drainage. Among grasses likely to be found on the tall-grass prairie are big bluestem, broomweed, buffalo grass, green needlegrass, panic grass, scurf-pea, and slender wheatgrass.

GARDENS

STATE	NICKNAME	ORIGIN
Illinois	The Prairie State	*Illini*, An Algonquin word meaning men or warriors.
Indiana	Hoosier State	Means "land of the Indians."
Iowa	Hawkeye State	A Dakota word variously translated as "dark and bloody ground," "meadow land," and "land of tomorrow."
Kansas	Sunflower State	Sioux word for "south wind people."
Michigan	Wolverine State	From two Indian words meaning "great lake."
Minnesota	North Star State Gopher State	From a Dakota Indian word meaning "sky-tinted water."
Missouri	Show Me State	Name of an Algonquin tribe; also means "muddy water," for Missouri River.
Nebraska	Cornhusker State	From Omaha or Otos Indian word meaning "broad water" or "flat river" describing the Platte River.
North Dakota	Peace Garden State	From the Dakota Tribe, meaning "allies."
Ohio	Buckeye State	Iroquois word for "fine" or "good river."
South Dakota	Coyote State Sunshine State	Same as North Dakota.
Wisconsin	Badger State	French corruption of an Indian word whose meaning is disputed.

FLOWER	BIRD	TREE
Native Violet	Cardinal	White Oak
Peony	Cardinal	Tulip Poplar
Wild Rose	Eastern Gold Finch	Oak
Native Sunflower	Western Meadowlark	Cottonwood
Apple Blossom	Robin	White Pine
Pink and White Lady's Slipper	Common Loon	Red Pine
Hawthorn	Bluebird	Dogwood
Goldenrod	Western Meadowlark	Cottonwood
Wild Prairie Rose	Western Meadowlark	American Elm
Scarlet Carnation	Cardinal	Buckeye
Pasque Flower	Ringnecked Pheasant	Black Hills Spruce
Wood Violet	Robin	Sugar Maple

Though they resemble black-eyed susans, coneflowers (right) have a distinctive shape: Their petals droop down from the centers. Yellow coneflowers like full sun and rich soil; they bloom in midsummer; there may be as many as thirty species of shooting stars (below) in the Midwest. All thrive in rich, damp soil.

A Rainbow of Native Wildflowers

Here are the best wildflowers to look for in the countryside, or plant on your own Heartland property.

Golden and Orange Flowers

Wild columbine (*Aquilegia canadensis*)

Milk-vetch (*Astragalus canadensis*)

Gaillardia (*Gaillardia aristata*)

Turk's-cap lily (*Lilium superbum*)

Dwarf evening primrose (*Oenothera missouriensis*)

Prairie buttercup (*Ranunculus rhomboideus*)

Yellow coneflower (*Ratibida pinnata*)

© Paul T. McMahon/Heartland Images

White Flowers

Wild onion (*Allium cernuum*)

Thimbleweed (*Anemone cylindrica*)

Black rattlepod (*Baptisia leucantha*)

Snow-in-summer (*Cerastium biebersteinii*)

Prairie larkspur (*Delphinium virescens*)

Shooting star (*Dodecatheon meadia*)

Bush clover (*Lespedeza capitata*)

Purple prairie clover (*Petalostemum candidum*)

© Derek Fell

Red and Pink Flowers

Columbine (*Aquilegia caerulea*)

Red milkweed (*Asclepias incarnata*)

Silky aster (*Aster sericeus*)

Queen-of-the-Prairie (*Filipendula rubra*)

Bergamot (*Monarda fistulosa*)

Prairie phlox (*Phlox pilosa*)

Catchfly (*Silene armeria*)

© Derek Fell

Queen of the Prairie (top) blooms in June and July, with colors varying from deep to light pink, depending on the plant. It prefers damp soil; most of 300-odd gentians found in the world are mountain plants, but bottle gentian (left) is suited to Heartland conditions.

© Derek Fell

Nobody sees a flower —really—it is so small—we haven't time—and to see takes time like to have a friend takes time.
—Georgia O'Keeffe

Blue, Violet, and Purple Flowers

Coneflower (*Echinacea purpurea*)

Pale purple coneflower (*Echinacea pallida*)

Bottle gentian (*Gentiana andrewsii*)

Wild iris (*Iris shrevei*)

Rough blazing star (*Liatris aspera*)

Dwarf blazing star (*Liatris cylindracea*)

Prairie blazing star (*Liatris pycnostachya*)

Spiderwort (*Tradescantia ohiensis*)

Ironweed (*Vernonia fasciculata*)

Birdsfood violet (*Viola pedata*)

THE POND GARDEN

On the farm the weather was the great fact, and men's affairs went on underneath it, as the streams creep under the ice.
—Willa Cather, My Antonia

A pond adds a whole new dimension to a yard and can be a garden in itself, filled with enchanting aquatic plants. Not only does it provide a reflective surface, it attracts a variety of birds and wildlife. Garden pools can be as simple as a hole lined with butyl rubber or PVC (polyvinyl chloride, a flexible plastic material). The lining is anchored around the rim with stones, and will last up to five years before needing to be replaced. Or pools can be more elaborate, complete with water pipes, pumps, fountains, and filters.

A natural pond can support a variety of water plants including water lilies, cattails, yellow flag, water hyacinths, and various grasses. Many of these will grow in a backyard pool, but certain bottom-rooting species such as water lilies must be potted shallowly in wood, clay, or plastic containers which are then placed underwater. Other plants float on top with roots dangling: water hyacinth, water lettuce, pennywort, watercress, and water hawthorn. And other water grasses act as oxygenators, absorbing carbon dioxide from decayed matter and animal waste, and releasing oxygen, which helps control the growth of algae. As these water plants establish themselves and oxygenate the water, fish can be brought into the pond.

When space is limited, Heartlanders contain their water gardens—in a caldron, wooden tub, ceramic crock, or wash tub. Tub gardens will work on balconies and patios, or in other situations where space is limited.

A mini ecosystem with lots of aesthetic appeal, a pond provides a habitat for toads, which help control the insect population. With a shallow ledge around its edge, a pool will provide a place for birds to drink and bathe. Be cautious about using pesticides. Chemical sprays will kill fish, butterflies, bees, and other small creatures. In *The Naturalist's Garden*, Ruth Ernst recommends that if your neighbor uses chemical sprays, you should site your pool behind sheltering shrubbery and put a wall (or your house) between the pool and the neighboring property. Lawn fertilizer is another no-no, as it will promote excessive algae growth.

THE ROCK GARDEN

A small group of devotees have always touted the rock garden as the paragon of low-maintenance beauty, especially in northern parts of the Heartland. With the trend toward perennials and the abundance of limestone and sandstone in the Midwest, rock gardens are a natural choice for Heartland gardeners.

Rock gardens do have some special requirements. First of all, they need well drained and aerated soil; clay is deadly to rock plants. Ideally, a rock garden should be oriented toward the east or the southeast so that plants can have some respite from the summer sun and heat. A rock wall or even just a stone trough on the patio can function as a "garden" as well. It's best to use local rock, if available. Talk to local experts (nursery workers, extension agents, other rock gardeners) about what plants will work best in your area.

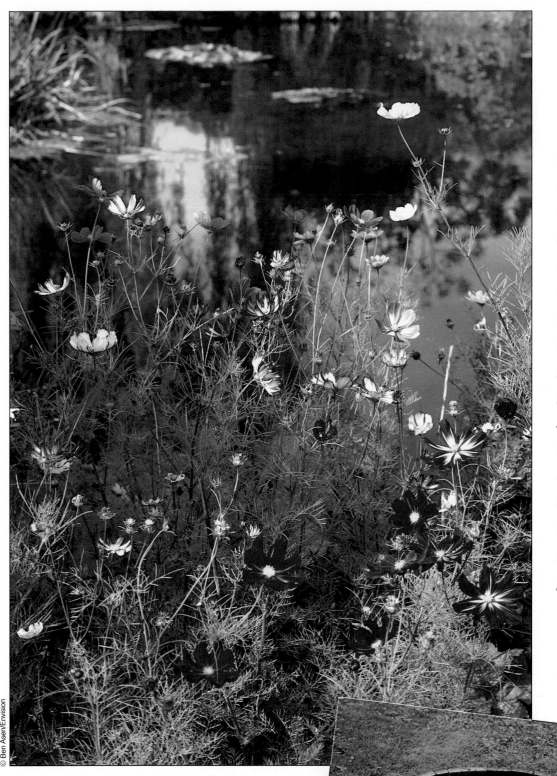

© Ben Asen/Envision

Wildflowers (top) spring up every summer along roadsides all over the Heartland. When planting a wildflower meadow, the key to success is using species native to your region; who says you need a pond to have a water garden? Follow the Japanese tradition of the miniature garden —in a tub (bottom). Certain hardy species of water lily thrive in even the coldest northern parts of the Midwest.

© Dick Keen/Envision

GARDENS